DISCARD

Lady Beware

Lady Beware

PETER ARNOLD

139656

DOUBLEDAY & COMPANY, INC.
Garden City, New York 1974

ISBN: 0-385-00951-8
Library of Congress Catalog Card Number 72–96271
Copyright © 1973, 1974, by Peter Arnold
All Rights Reserved
Printed in the United States of America
First Edition

To Jeremy
In hopes that his
America will be safe

ACKNOWLEDGMENTS

A great many men and women were very generous with their time and advice, and I would like to thank them for helping to make this book possible.

My thanks go to child psychotherapist Patricia Powers of Los Angeles; Dr. Robert Alan Cole, a psychiatrist in Los Angeles; and Mr. and Mrs. Maurice Hattem of the People's Protective League, Canoga Park, California. Also, officials of the Department of Human Resources, Simi, California.

Police experts from around the country answered my many questions and volunteered additional information. I would like to thank the following for their co-operation: Edward M. Davis, Chief of Police of Los Angeles; C. R. Gain, Chief of Police of Oakland; and Jerry V. Wilson, Chief of Police of Washington, D.C. Also, top officials of the Federal Bureau of Investigation, and of the police departments of Ann Arbor, Atlanta, Chicago, Dallas, Denver, Des Moines, Detroit, Las Vegas, Miami, Newton (Massachusetts), Philadelphia, San Francisco, and Seattle.

In addition, several men and women of the New York Police Department were very helpful, including Detective Larry Carr,

Policewoman Mary Glatzle, Policeman Bob Lucente, and many others. My thanks also go to Sergeant Edward Powers for setting up several interviews and offering his own valuable information.

Parole agents arranged most of my interviews with convicted felons and gave me important insights into them. Although I am unable to credit these parole agents by name, I deeply appreciate their vital contribution to this book.

For over two years, some dedicated men and women of the Los Angeles Police Department guided my research. I thank Sergeant Bud Carr; Investigator Connie Davies; Sergeant Elizabeth Eggleston; Sergeant Barbara Guarino; officer Ken Harris; Sergeant Genevieve Hauck; Lieutenant Frank Isbell; Policewoman Cindy Miller; Lieutenant Glen Sherman; and Captain Jack R. Wilson.

My special thanks go to Lieutenant Jim Motherway of the New York Police Department, who gave me a personal look at the men and women behind a unique crime-prevention program.

And last, my deep appreciation goes to Sergeant Lee Kirkwood of the Los Angeles Police Department. Sergeant Kirkwood first told me of the need for this book, gave repeated advice throughout the writing, and then proofread the final copy.

Every effort has been made to produce an accurate book. If any errors remain, they are my responsibility.

PETER ARNOLD

CONTENTS

Lady Beware

1

Crime Prevention

In New York City after dark, Central Park West is an unsafe street. Yet seated on a bench was a petite woman in her twenties who appeared to be asleep.

She just sat there unmoving, perhaps unaware of the people who walked by her. Some paid her no attention. Others stopped and looked. She was an "easy mark" in the darkness, her pocketbook by her thigh. Young men took the most interest, including one bare-chested youth who wanted some sex and told her so.

But she said nothing. She didn't even budge. When a junkie hits up with heroin, they say he can't get his chin off his chest. That's how she looked—sitting up with her chin on her chest. Perhaps her sunglasses hid the sick eyes of an addict.

Other men came and went but a few remained in the distance. About thirty yards to her right, an effeminate man in maroon talked with passers-by. A straight-looking man sat close to the fellow with the lisp. About forty yards to the woman's left sat a black man dressed in a football shirt and shorts, twirling a cane. Every once in a while, the black man would look over at a white guy in a straw hat. Then they'd look over at the woman.

Across the wide street, a handsome man with blond hair stood watching everything: the street, the sidewalk, the men, and the woman. He tried to lounge casually against a building but he was nervous.

Some forty-five minutes after the bare-chested youth talked to her of sex, the street was empty. So was the sidewalk. The guy in maroon and his friend said nothing, the black man with the cane and the white man in the straw hat sat silently. It was quiet. The woman remained sitting.

Then a man came walking by in a hurry. He had some important business on his mind so he strode right past the woman. Then he stopped several feet from her left side. He'd changed his mind: she was his important business.

Behind the bench she sat on was a wall three feet high. On the other side of the wall was Central Park. The man moved quickly to the wall and, with his back to it, started slowly toward her. She remained motionless.

But not him. He sneaked along the wall five feet from her . . . three feet . . . right behind her.

He looked around: no cars, no pedestrians, all quiet.

His hand came over the bench toward her and her pocketbook. Slowly. Then, quickly, he grabbed it and turned to run.

In a flash, the woman jumped up, took a loaded gun from the folds of her dress, pointed it at him and commanded, "Stop!"

The guy in maroon and his friend raced down toward them; the black man and the guy in the straw hat raced up; and the blond man from across the street ran over.

The handcuffs were out, the guns were drawn, and the man was led away to an unmarked police car. He was under arrest.

The woman who sat on the bench waiting to be robbed or mugged or stabbed is Policewoman Mary Glatzle. They call her Muggable Mary. The blond man who waited nervously across the street is her boss, Lieutenant Jim Motherway. He and Mary and the four others (the fellow in maroon, his friend, the black man, and the white guy in the straw hat) are all part of the New York Police Department's Citywide Anticrime Section.

In this book you will hear from Policewoman Glatzle, Lieutenant Motherway, and several other men and women of the New York Police Department. Out on the West Coast, you will hear from Sergeant Lee Kirkwood and Officer Ken Harris, two experts from the Los Angeles Police Department. Sergeant Barbara Guarino and Investigator Connie Davies, both mothers and policewomen in L.A., will relate their experiences acting as decoys for rapists and sex perverts. And Investigator Cindy Miller, who works undercover in the vice rackets, will tell you the technique she uses to keep herself from harm.

In New York, in Los Angeles, in cities and suburbs and towns all across the country, police personnel are fighting crime. Their work is vital to you, wherever you live. According to the FBI *Uniform Crime Reports—1972* (the latest complete summary available), a total of 5.9 million crimes were reported to the FBI by local police. Serious crimes decreased 2 per cent, yet property loss was more than $2 billion. Robberies dropped 3 per cent and burglaries dropped 1 per cent, but murder was up 5 per cent, assaults increased 7 per cent, and rapes were up 11 per cent. According to these statistics, your risk of becoming a victim of crime is about one in thirty-five.

Although I'll be using FBI figures throughout this book, they are frequently too low. Some experts say that half to three quarters of all larcenies, burglaries, assaults, and rapes are never reported to the police. Among the many facts these figures do accurately show, however, is a trend of crime moving out of the large cities and into the suburbs. Though your risks of becoming a victim of crime are twice as high in cities of over 250,000 people as opposed to suburbs, in 1972 suburban crime increased 2 per cent. Rural crime was up 4 per cent.

Some people look at figures like these and think, "Oh, it will never happen to me." Others take the opposite view and react, "If one in thirty-five is a victim, then someone among my family, friends, and neighbors is going to get it; maybe me." Neither view is realistic. No one is immune from crime for, in fact, everyone is a potential victim. Whether or not you or your loved ones will be victimized depends largely on where and how you live, work and play, plus how you act.

This is a crime-prevention book. Its basic purpose is to help you prevent crime before it happens to you, your children, and others you love. If you have already been burglarized, robbed, mugged, assaulted, raped, or your child has been molested, then this book can help you prevent a recurrence.

If nothing has happened so far, great! The following pages will help you keep it that way.

You will find the advice of Los Angeles Chief of Police Edward M. Davis, Oakland Chief of Police C. R. Gain, and Washington D.C. Chief of Police Jerry V. Wilson. Other police experts not already mentioned include men and women of the police departments of Ann Arbor, Atlanta, Chicago, Dallas, Denver, Des Moines, Detroit, Las Vegas, Miami, Newton (Massachusetts), Philadelphia, San Francisco, and Seattle.

Also to help prevent you from becoming a victim of crime, you can learn from the experiences of women who were victims. Some of these women you will hear from have had their houses or apartments burglarized, their pocketbooks or cars stolen. Other women will discuss being robbed, assaulted, or raped, or the molestation of their children.

Then there is a very different type of expert whose words you will read: the mugger, burglar, auto thief, rapist, and child molester. They will discuss the ways they operate and the ways they think you can avoid becoming a victim.

But let me say right off that no experts and no amount of information can guarantee you 100 per cent protection. Basically it's a matter of being aware of the various problems and acting in your own behalf.

This reminds me of a humorous incident. Parole agents set up most of my interviews with convicted robbers, rapists, and other felons. One parole agent asked me to come to his Santa Monica home on a Sunday afternoon to meet a rapist and a child molester. I really wanted to meet a rapist and a child molester, but I told him that I usually spend Sunday afternoon with my wife and child. "Well," he answered, "bring them along."

In this case, my wife and little boy would have been perfectly safe. Nevertheless, they stayed home. They could avoid this situation and they did. But many times people can't or don't want to avoid situations of potential danger. Other times, they may be unaware that any danger exists.

Lady Beware tries to get you to beware of certain situations by first making you aware of them. Hopefully, you already know and practice certain crime-prevention measures. The case histories from police, from victims, and from offenders will teach you some others. You will not, however, find any gory or terrifying details of crimes in this book. My purpose is not to alarm you, it is to alert you. You will read some tragic stories and some funny ones, too. There are even some case histories in the following pages that are both humorous and sad.

The headline stories about robbers and rapists have been left for the newspapers where you can read their chilling descriptions easily enough. This book contains true stories that seldom if ever make any page in the newspapers but happen every day, many times a day. Eleven serious crimes occur each minute.

With the exception of a few officers who are involved in undercover operations, the names of all police personnel are true. The names of the victims mentioned in the chapter on hitchhiking are true, but all others are fictitious. All of the offenders asked that their names be changed and I have complied.

Whether they're on the right side of the law, the wrong side of the law, or caught in the middle, this book is about people. People cause crime, careless people sustain crime, cautious people prevent crime. The emphasis here is on the latter.

Locks, alarms, and other hardware are an important component of crime prevention but they are not the major part. You are. All discussions of equipment have been reduced to the simplest terms and discussed in the clearest language I can manage. There are no highly technical details to bog you down.

You may be technically oriented or you may not. I don't know. But I do know that every single day there are many times when you are vulnerable to crime. Whether you are a teen-ager or a grandmother, wealthy or poor, beautiful or plain, just about any woman is a better target for crime than just about any man.

Most women are physically weaker than most offenders (most of whom are men). Most women carry pocketbooks that are readily accessible. Most women (and men) are busy thinking about school or work or the children or other problems and not thinking about the chance of being a victim. And all women, whether they are five-year-old girls or eighty-five-year-old ladies, all women are potential victims of sex crimes.

While Muggable Mary Glatzle was sitting on the bench on Central Park West, forty-five minutes elapsed when little happened. My heart was beating fast much of the time as I watched this five-foot-two, 108-pound woman with big brown eyes. She was the bait for a coming crime. When it was over and we were all in the precinct station, I asked her what she thought about during that forty-five-minute period. As is her manner, Mary answered very quickly, "My son's going to be four tomorrow and I was wondering which was my best recipe for a birthday cake."

That's part of her story. When we talked further, I found that Mary wears sunglasses at night so no one can see her eyes. They move around a lot, looking everywhere. Why? Because she's scared. And she feigned sleep because there have been several stabbings in the area where she was sitting. If she appeared to be asleep, she figured there would be less reason to stab her.

Mary knows what she's doing. Even while she's thinking of recipes, she's practicing crime prevention. When she's off duty, she's very careful where and how and when she walks and drives, how she leaves her home, how she lives inside it. And she's very careful about her four-year-old son.

In a very special way, Mary and her associates practice crime prevention every day. You can practice it, too. And if you can deter a crime happening to you, you save yourself time and money and lots of hurt and anguish. The following pages will give you detailed information on what to do in a confrontation with a burglar, robber, rapist, or child molester. You will also find alternatives on what to do after one of these crimes has occurred.

But every effort will be made to let you know how you can keep yourself and those you love from becoming a victim before it happens. In the words of Los Angeles Chief of Police Edward M. Davis, "The function of first priority is prevention."

2

Outside Your Home

How often are you alone?

A little of the time? Some of the time? Most of the time? Or perhaps, as some women tell me, not enough of the time!

Many women find themselves almost always in the company of children, so let me ask my question another way. How often are you either alone or in the company of other women or children without any men around?

Think about it.

Whether you're in your teens, twenties, thirties, middle or later years, the chances are you spend more time alone, with other women, or with children, than you do with men. You are one of today's women and you are independent, you are mobile, you are doing things on your own. Since men are seldom around, *you* have to watch out for yourself.

And if you have children, *you* must also watch out for your kids.

The police are overburdened, your man is often off on his business, you are taking care of your things, violent crimes are way up and so are your responsibilities—to yourself and those you love.

There is no way around our crime problems. The only way to be safer is to know as much as possible about burglars and burglary, robbers and robbery, auto thieves and auto thefts, child molesters and child molesting, rapists and rapes. Then, after you know, you must think and act for yourself.

BURGLARS

Burglaries are the most frequent crime today. There were 2.3 million burglaries last year, one every thirteen seconds; $722 million worth of property was taken with an average dollar loss of $308 per burglary. For most of us, a loss of $308 would be pretty hard to sustain.

Do you have insurance that covers loss of property due to burglary? If so, find out exactly what it covers, how much of a loss you will sustain because of depreciation, and if you will sustain it all if there is no evidence of forced entry.

But, of course, insurance isn't the answer. Prevention is. Only 19 per cent of the burglary offenses were solved last year.

Let's start by talking about burglars themselves. They are young. Almost all (83 per cent) are under twenty-five and half (51 per cent) are under eighteen. Almost all are male, with only about 5 per cent female. You can pretty much count on his being fairly thin and fast on his feet; thin so he can climb through windows, fast so he can run quickly with your possessions.

Another thing you can count on: he's scared. When he's in your house or apartment, he's scared. Bill is a sixteen-year-old high school student. He is also a burglar. This is what he told the police:

> When I was twelve, me and another kid snuck into this girl we knew's home. Ellen. That was her name. We saw her mother leave and we thought, "Maybe we can get in." The front door was locked but not the back, so in we went. Our hearts were beating like mad. Man! It was the first time for both of us and we were nervous. We were in the kitchen when Ellen came out of a room.
>
> My friend knew her pretty well so he started talking a mile a minute, you know, talking like mad and shoving his hands

in and out of his pockets. But me, hell, I just went into a bed-room, found her mother's purse, and took out a few bills. I came back to the kitchen and there they were eating some cookies. I had some too.

After that, I'd go into homes whenever I wanted. I'd be walking down the street and see someone leave so me and some friends would just walk in and get some stuff. It was easy. A snap. Other times, we'd steal bicycles.

When I got my license early this year, I really started haul-ing it in. Just driving around, looking for people leaving home. Sometimes, we'd know people were out so in we'd go. It was so easy, you know?

It was easy for Bill, until the police tracked him down. His story is common among burglars. Denver police experts talk about them this way: "The residential burglar is an opportunist. He wants to gain entry quickly, quietly, without being seen and with as little effort as possible."

Another young man, I'll call him Jim, also fits this description. Jim differs from Bill, however, because Jim never burglarizes homes of people he doesn't know. He doesn't strike out at strangers, but goes after neighbors, relatives, and his own family. He also acts on opportunity and may even have his own key to a home. And he's after money and goods but also a thrill or a chance to get back at someone. Jim's story comes from the police:

My old man kicked me out of the house. I was seventeen. He said, "You're old enough to be on your own so get." So I got. Big deal.

But hell, I didn't have any money, not much anyway. And I left so fast I couldn't take my things with me.

One day I went back into my home. I knew he [Jim's father] wouldn't be there so I took some of my things. Then I saw my old man's guitar. Man, I loved that guitar but he'd never let me play it. So I took it. I bet he was mad.

I went back some other times to get some money and things but he didn't have much. Then I figured I had some uncles who were loaded so I went to their homes.

After a while, I was in pretty good shape. No one knew where I lived so they couldn't get me and it sure beat work-

ing. So I kind of branched out. I started hitting my neighbors.
I knew when they were home and when they were out but it
was dumb. They knew me and they knew where I lived. One
of them saw me wearing his pants.

Bill, Jim, and other young burglars accounted for about 200,000
burglary arrests last year. You can bet many other youths did the
same sort of thing but were never arrested. Together, these young
burglars comprise some 51 per cent of the burglary problem.

But neither Bill nor Jim nor their confederates are hooked on
drugs. Some burglars who are addicts are under eighteen, most are
older, but whatever their age, a burglar who is a drug addict is
very dangerous. He is called a "hype" and commits about 30 per
cent of all burglaries.

A kid like Bill or Jim can be dangerous if you catch him
burglarizing your home. A hype is always dangerous. He burglarizes to get money for his habit. When he needs $25 or $50 or $100
a day for heroin, he *must* have it. One way or another, he'll get
that money by stealing cash or goods that he can quickly turn into
cash.

C.T. is a hype. He is a handsome man in his early thirties, an
up-tight kind of guy with a dark intensity about him. He can become very excited when he talks and you know he could be big
trouble when he needs a fix. He is now on a state program for drug
rehabilitation. I spoke with him recently and recorded these words:

> I'd tried stores and plants but nothing beats houses. I'd
> cruise along looking for an open garage with no car inside or
> a dark house with only a front light on.
>
> [How did you get into a home?] Usually, I'd just walk in
> through a back door or a side door. Once in a while through
> the front door or a window.
>
> [Did you ever force your way in?] Oh yeah, sometimes. If
> things were locked up tight and I had to.
>
> [What do you mean, if you had to?] Well, you know, if I
> had to have money. That was pretty often but I usually could
> find someplace to get in easy.
>
> [Have you ever gone into a home and found someone
> there?] No.

[What would happen if you needed money, broke into a home, and found someone inside?] I don't know. If I needed a fix, I'd get some money. If they saw me or got in my way or anything, I'd get the money. It's as simple as that.

Obviously, you don't want to be in C.T.'s way when he needs a fix. And you don't want your children around him, either. The best way to avoid him is to keep him out in the first place.

Any burglar, C.T. included, will take one look at your home and decide one of three things: to take a longer look, to come back later and enter, or to move on to an easier home. The first impression of your home is what counts. And please don't think your home is not worth a second look to a burglar. Any and every home contains money or goods that can be turned into money.

The poorest homes are very often burglarized. Slum homes, ghetto tenements, tiny apartments, any and every home is a potential target because every home has watches and clocks, small appliances, a hi-fi or TV, cash or jewelry or guns or antiques.

The chances are that a burglar has walked or driven by your home already. This fact depends upon where you live and the incidence of crime in your area. Check with your local police. If you don't already know it, they will probably tell you there have been burglaries nearby.

But there is one vital fact that may prevent your home from being burglarized. That fact is *you,* your presence in the house or apartment. Sergeant Lee Kirkwood, a veteran of the Burglary Division and now with the Crime Prevention Section of the Los Angeles Police Department, explains the situation this way:

A burglar doesn't want to meet people, he wants to avoid them. He'll look the home over very carefully. If no one appears to be inside, he may walk up close and listen for any sounds of people. He may even ring the doorbell. He doesn't want to meet people because he doesn't want to be delayed, and he doesn't want to be seen.

There are some very important precautions you must take before you go away for a trip. These are covered in Chapter 7. You are, however, more liable to be burglarized when you step out for an hour or two, or for a day, or for coffee next door. Why? Because when you leave for just a little while, you are apt to be careless.

When you are home during the day, the shades or curtains or blinds are open. The radio or hi-fi or TV is on or the vacuum cleaner, the dishwasher, the egg beater, or some other appliance is working. The heater may be on if it's cold or the air conditioning or a fan if it's hot. The clothes may be on a line outside or small toys may lie around or a car may wait in the driveway or the garage.

When you are home at night, all of these sights and noises plus several lights on inside and out indicate that you are inside. But when you're away, even if for a very short while, it's very quiet and still. No one is seen or heard because no one is there.

So we now have two factors that interest the burglar. First, that your home, like every other, has some goods that he can turn into cash and maybe you have some cash, too. And secondly, no one appears to be home. If you combine this with easy access, then sooner or later you can count on being burglarized.

Easy access is provided by doors that are left open, left unlocked, or locked with ineffective mechanisms. Easy access is also provided by windows that are either left open or left closed but not locked. Screens provide no protection against burglary. One woman claimed to police that although she left a window open, there was a screen on it. Of course the burglar simply cut the screen and climbed in.

One unlocked door or one open or unsecured window is all a burglar needs.

Then there are people who think that the best way to let a burglar know they are home is to leave a door wide open. The reasoning here is that since no one would leave a door wide open unless they were home, the burglar will realize this and stay away. That is pretty poor reasoning. Some people actually do leave doors open when they go out, and some doors don't lock properly and swing open by themselves.

More importantly, even if you are in the backyard or busy up-stairs or down in the cellar, a burglar may enter your home because a door is open. The temptation and the opportunity are too great.

It can take only a minute or two for a young burglar to see an open door, run in, grab one or two things, and run out. He may not even have been looking for trouble. But he found it. And the person who left the door open helped the burglar.

Now we have the three major elements burglars look for before they burglarize: money or goods, no one home and little chance of being seen or caught, and fast entrance and exit.

That's the case with some 80 per cent of burglars. The remainder are the pros. A pro doesn't want to meet you, either. But he'll take more time in choosing his target and he'll be more organized both on the job and in the disposal of your possessions. Most of the time he'll look like he fits right into your neighborhood. For example, if you live in an exclusive area, he'll rent himself a Cadillac, put on a new suit, and appear to be an insurance agent or a realtor. Then if he's stopped in the street or meets someone in a home, he'll go into a credible routine about insurance or real estate and apologize for being at the wrong address.

Some pros act alone, others work in pairs or groups. Some make their way across the country, burglarizing homes and stealing cars as they go. Others use moving vans that they back up to a home after they've observed the occupants leaving, then move everything out. Since they dress in the uniforms of a moving company, neighbors seldom ask questions.

Very few burglars, however, pick locks. That takes too much time and is unnecessary since so many people are careless. Instead, the pros (as well as the hypes and some of the kids) will carry simple tools like jackknives, crowbars, screw drivers, or maybe only credit cards or pieces of Celluloid. Many inadequate locks can be "loided" by working a credit card or Celluloid strip between the latch and the doorjamb, snapping back the latch and unlocking the door.

More than other burglars, the pros love to boast. At least that's my experience with them. Roger is the name I'm giving to one professional I met. Tall, thin, and about thirty-five, he claims to have hit "several thousand" homes. He's a very cocky guy, proud of his ability to "break into any home," but, as you'll see, he goes only after easy marks:

I'm an investor. You smile but it's true. I invest my time and skill in other people's goods. I take risks to make a profit, and I do profit. Or at least I did until I quit.

I'd look at a home and decide what the risk is. If it's going to take a lot of my time to get in, then why bother? See, I like to get in, take things, and get out in three minutes. Three minutes. That's all it used to take me.

See, the longer it takes to get in and the longer I'm inside, the greater risk of getting seen, or of someone returning home.

Course sometimes, if I'm doing well, real well, I'll take on a home with dogs and alarms and locked doors and windows. Sure. I like a challenge, like everybody else. I know ways around dogs and alarms and locks. Sure I do. But they take time. They increase my risk. So most of the time, I'm very businesslike.

Unfortunately, much of Roger's boasting is corroborated by his rap sheet. He may not have a record of thousands of hits, but he probably did pull off substantially more than one hundred jobs. There may be no way for you absolutely to stop a pro like Roger, but there are many measures that can deter him and, especially, his less-experienced confederates.

BURGLARY PREVENTION

Every burglar wants to have it easy. The youth wants it to be "a snap," the hype wants to get "in and out fast," and the pro wants "low risk/high return." Show him your home is not easy but *hard*. Show him that you're home, show him that your home is secure, and show him that he will be caught if he burglarizes your home.

How can you do all of these things just from the appearance of the outside of your home? By being cautious.

A little over half of all burglaries occur during daylight hours, evidence that burglars want to be in your home when you are out. The burglar will walk or drive by your house or apartment. If the garage door is open and no car is inside, you can bet the burglar will stop and look twice. Leaving your garage door open gives the burglar more information than just the vital fact that you're probably not home. As one burglar told me, "If people are careless about the garage door, they're careless about locking their doors."

The open garage door also gives access to tools, lawnmowers, ladders, or whatever else you keep in the garage. And it also gives a good hiding place to a mugger or rapist who can wait for your return. So keep your garage door shut and locked.

"But that's a bother. It's much easier to open the door, back out, and go on your way, especially when you'll be right back." That's the way some people think. If you're one of them, you're vulnerable.

If you've got about $200, you can buy an automatic garage-door opener that works either by a special signal from your car or, preferably, by inserting a plastic card in a slot near your garage. The automatic garage-door opener will save time and some struggling with heavy garage doors. More importantly, because it's very convenient to just push a button or insert a card, you'll be more apt to shut the garage door every time you use it.

But $200 may be too costly. You might make the garage door easier to close by having a good system of springs installed if the old ones are rusty.

While it is necessary to shut your garage door, that may do little good if you don't also lock it with a strong lock. The single lock on overhead garage doors is inadequate to keep intruders from prying up the other end and crawling in. Add another bolt and a quality padlock to the other side.

A quality padlock is made of hardened steel and has at least a $\frac{9}{32}$-inch shackle (though heavier shackles offer additional security). It has a double locking mechanism (heel and toe), has a five-pin tumbler, and has a key-retaining feature that prevents removing the key until the padlock is locked.

You may want to add a top center hasp and use your padlock with it. If so, the hasp must be of hardened steel and installed with carriage bolts through the door. Large washers should be used on the inside, and, after the nuts are secured, you should deface the threads of the bolt ends with a hammer to keep the nuts from being removed.

A third alternative is to install cane bolts inside the door, but these are operable only from the inside.

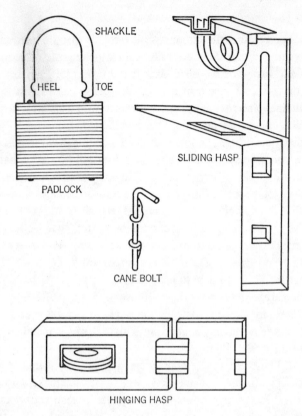

SHACKLE

HEEL | TOE

PADLOCK

SLIDING HASP

CANE BOLT

HINGING HASP

At the same time you increase the security of your garage door, paint any garage windows and cover any vents from the inside to keep someone from looking in.

If you have two cars but only one is being used, some police officials advise parking the unused car outside the garage or outside the home to give the appearance that you are home or that you have company. If you take this advice, be sure to lock your car. Otherwise, it may be stolen.

And there's another problem with this particular advice. Roger, the professional burglar, would reason that if the unused car is small, the family might all have piled into the big car and left. In other words, a small car parked in front of the home would pique his interest.

You'll have to decide for yourself whether or not to park an unused car in front of your home or outside your garage. I suggest leaving it in the garage.

We're still out in the street with a burglar who is looking at your home during the day. If he sees small, inexpensive toys around it, the chances are you're home. But if there are bicycles left in front or at the side or in back and he sees them, he'll probably figure that whether you're home or not you're careless about your locks. How does he arrive at that conclusion? Unlocked bikes, like unlocked garage doors, are tip-offs to noncautious people and to homes that are easy marks.

Shades or drapes or blinds that are closed during the day probably mean that no one is home. People usually like to see out and let the sunshine in, unless the sun is too bright or they are sleeping late. Otherwise, drawn window coverings are a solid sign to a burglar that no one is there.

The burglar is now taking a second, closer look. He starts toward your home. He may look like a salesman carrying a briefcase or he may look like a delivery boy. Whatever his appearance, he will not attract attention to himself by looking disreputable or suspicious. He will not wear dirty clothes and need a shave. He will look like a neighborhood kid or a workman or a businessman.

He's walking toward your home and he doesn't see you. But maybe he can hear you even if you're not home. How? Inexpensive automatic timers (they cost from $5.00 to $10.00, but fancy ones will run to $100) can turn on radios or TVs or fans. You won't even need to use timers if you put on a radio before you leave. Keep the volume low so it won't disturb your neighbors and place the radio near the front of the home where a burglar can hear it.

Because they don't want to meet anyone when they have illegally intruded into a home, most burglars will not break into a home if a radio or some other noise is heard. They just won't take the chance.

But the burglar we're talking about wants to make sure no one's home. He goes up and rings your bell. No one is home so no one will come to the door. What can you do?

Well, it is possible to have a tape recorder rigged to the doorbell so that, when the bell rings, the tape recorder plays a message like "I can't come to the door. My child has chicken pox and the doctor says not to let anyone in." Honestly now, I don't know anyone who has done this, but it's not a bad idea.

Since no one is coming to the door, you have to do something. The radio that's playing may mean someone is busy in another part of the house, but that's a pretty weak defense. Instead, show him that your home is secure, that it will be hard to break into. Let him see that the doors are sturdy and are shut and locked with tough locks. Show him that the windows are either closed and locked with solid window locks, or open too little for him to climb through and secured in position in such a way that they can't be opened further. (Chapter 3 discusses locks and other security devices in detail.)

You've done your best to show him that you're home and that your home is secure. But he's still thinking about breaking in. Given enough time and enough knowledge, a pro can break in to just about any home.

But there is still another line of defense: good signs. Certain signs on your front door and side door and back door will tell him he's liable to get caught if he intrudes into this home and if he takes some of its possessions. These good signs include warnings that a dog is present or that the house is equipped with a burglar-alarm system. A tiny minority of professional burglars boasted to me that they love it when people advertise about dogs and alarms. That way, brag these burglars, they know what to look out for.

Only a tiny minority will want to bother with dogs or alarms, however, and the vast majority will decide to move on to an easy home. Dogs and alarms are not foolproof, but they do take time and effort to circumvent and the burglar might not succeed. So if you have a dog or an alarm system, advertise it on all your exterior doors, not just the front. Even if they don't have a dog or an alarm, some people put up signs announcing them. Many locksmiths carry phony burglar-alarm decals and you might feel safer displaying them. I don't recommend them, however, as you'll probably fool only yourself.

Dogs and alarms are detection systems that might also be deterrents. So might systems of marking possessions with personal identifying numbers: Operation Identification or the Computer Identification System. Or there are warning decals stating that all items have been marked for police identification. Your local police department has these decals for your doors.

Alarms and property identification systems will be discussed in Chapters 3 and 5. Right now we're talking solely about deterrents that are seen from outside your home. It is often hard to prove the effectiveness of any deterrent. Additionally, certain types of possessions are not susceptible to marking (such as money, jewelry, and many antiques).

But I've talked with twelve different ex-burglars and close to twice that number of burglary investigators. The consensus is: put up as many potential deterrents as possible.

On the next page are samples of some decals you can put on your doors. (I have not shown the phoney alarm decal because that would give it away to a burglar, nor have I included any of the many true alarm-system signs.)

At the other extreme, there are signs that entice and welcome burglars. There is one sign that attracts muggers and rapists and can be found on houses and apartments all over the country. It can also be found on mailboxes and apartment house directories. It is a nameplate that spells out the fact that the occupant is a woman.

Never have your marital status or your first or middle names on your nameplate. Miss (or Mrs. or Ms.) Jane Ellen Logan should immediately be changed to J. Logan. And if no one with your last name lives in the area, just have your last name, such as Logan, on the nameplate. This is a simple, inexpensive task that is *vital* to your safety.

Other signs entice burglars, though, of course, the intention is far different. One is a note that says a person is out to lunch, has gone shopping, or will be back at a certain time. Whatever its exact contents, its message is that no one is home. And that's great news for a burglar.

Some people even announce in the newspaper that their homes will be vacant. An event like a confirmation, bar mitzvah, wedding, or funeral that is mentioned in the paper tells a burglar no one will be at home during certain hours. If you want this information given to the public, then hire some trustworthy person to spend a few hours inside your home.

You don't want to leave valuable furs, other clothing or rugs on the clothes line unless you are there and watching them. Otherwise,

WARNING

all **VALUABLES**
MARKED for
IDENTIFICATION
and can be
TRACED by

POLICE

Courtesy of

COAST
AND SOUTHERN FEDERAL SAVINGS
AND LOAN ASSOCIATION

WARNING

ALL VALUABLE ITEMS ON THESE
PREMISES ARE REGISTERED WITH
THE DALLAS POLICE DEPARTMENT'S
COMPUTER IDENTIFICATION SYSTEM.

TX_____

YOUR *Independent* AGENT
Insurance
SERVES YOU FIRST

We Have Joined...

OPERATION
IDENTIFICATION

All Items of value on these
premises have been marked for
ready identification by Law
Enforcement Agencies.

WM. F. QUINN - CHIEF

INSURANCE AGENTS OF NEWTON

you are dangling bait in front of any thief who happens by. In winter, you won't want to leave foot or tire tracks in the snow that only show people leaving. Instead, walk or drive back and forth to indicate that some people have returned.

And one of the very worst practices that so many people still perform is leaving keys outside the home. Supposedly hidden under the mat, over the door, behind a milk bottle, under a flower pot, or on a window ledge, these and other secret places are not at all secret. No key should be hidden outside your house or apartment because even the first-time burglar knows the hiding places.

On the other hand, it is a good idea to have a key outside your home in case you misplace your key or you want to let someone inside your home before you return. The answer? Give a spare key to a trusted neighbor. And, for the friend coming to see you before you return, leave no note that the neighbor has a key (for that will tell a burglar you're not at home). Tell your friend over the phone or in person to see the neighbor for a key. And tell the neighbor, too.

If you leave a key near the door, the burglar will be in your home in a second. But if there's no key and the front door is locked, yet he's sure no one's home, he'll probably walk around to the back. Since the front door is usually in view of the street, he'll look for a door or window that can conceal him while he works it open and enters.

Tall shrubbery, high wooden fences, or brick walls around a home give a thief the time he needs. So do tall plants near doors and windows. If it's possible to trim your shrubbery, do so. But if you want to have privacy from passers-by and neighbors, please realize that you also have less security. A dog that has free run of the entire yard (not confined to one area where an offender can get to him or go around him) can help balance this deficiency. Strong outdoor lights can also help at night.

A little less than half of all residential burglaries occur at night and almost all of these are committed before midnight. Most people who are out for the evening are home by twelve so that's when the great majority of burglars retire. What attracts them at night? No lights on. Or no lights on inside and only a front or back-door light on outside. Starting right at dusk, if lights don't go on, no one is home.

Think about it. Of course some lights would be on if it were dark and you were eating supper or watching TV or doing a chore. But if you were out and didn't take a minute beforehand to be cautious, you wouldn't put any lights on inside and might only put a front light on outside.

Larry is about average height but very thin. He's a very reserved person, in part because he's been a heroin addict for twenty-one years. He's spent ten years in prison, many months in jail, and is now trying to straighten himself out on methadone. Most of his years in prison were for burglary. He pulled "hundreds and hundreds" of jobs:

> [Was there any one thing that told you and your two partners to go past one house and look for another?] Lights. If there were lights on, we'd go on. If no lights, then we look around, knock at the front door. If they answer, I make up some story about being at the wrong home and leave. If no one comes to the front, I go around back and cut a screen.
>
> I never went into a home if there were any lights on. Or any radio or TV. Never.

Lights inside and outside the home are an excellent measure for burglary prevention.

If you won't be home until after dark, have an automatic timer put on some interior lights. Lamps on in two different rooms are fine, but make sure the light can be seen from the most likely place a burglar will view your home: the street. A woman who is alone will do well to keep some lights on in several rooms even when she *is* at home. This will give the impression that others are with her.

Outside lights should cover all entrances to the house—front, side and rear—plus the garage door. It costs only pennies a night to burn 60-watt light bulbs at necessary points around your house and they will make even a professional think twice. Light is the enemy of crime.

The best position for these exterior lights is under the eaves where they are hard for an offender to assault. An automatic timer or a photo-electric cell can turn them on. And, incidentally, these lights can add a dramatic quality to your home.

Outside lights should be on from dusk to dawn. It's also wise to have at least one interior light on all night. A bathroom, kitchen, study, or other light that can be seen from the outside will give the impression that someone is up, no matter what the hour.

The crime-prevention measures visible outside your home will tell almost all burglars, as well as most muggers and rapists, that your home is not worth bothering with. But a very few burglars are super-pros, the kind that make Roger (the man who boasts of "thousands and thousands" of hits) look like a kid. J.G. is a super-burglar. His story comes of talks with several policemen:

> J.G. graduated Phi Beta Kappa from a prestige eastern university. He had a great future ahead of him as a lawyer, a field he liked. But nothing gave him the challenge of burglary. He loved to outwit the police.
>
> To find out what the police were doing, he'd steal the radio equipment out of police vehicles. That way he'd know how close they were to catching him and he'd get away. He'd also steal equipment from private citizens.
>
> One night he started over the wall of a mansion and suddenly noticed that he'd already tripped a silent burglar alarm. That got him mad. He left, came back the next night, and not only disengaged the alarm system, but stole it so he could figure out how it worked.
>
> Among his other exploits were breaking into the homes of the security head of a major industrial plant and burglarizing the home of a deputy chief of police.
>
> More often, his time would be spent performing a "milk run." In the middle of the night, while the occupants of the homes were asleep, he'd break into one house after another, steal money, jewelry, and electronic equipment such as TVs and stereos, and hide them outside in the bushes. Then he'd work his way down the street, hitting home after home. Before dawn, he'd steal a car, drive slowly up the street, and pile the merchandise in.

J.G.'s story is fascinating but sad. He could have led a worthwhile, productive life. He could have defended criminals instead of becoming one. I'm told he now realizes this as he serves his term in a penitentiary. Time simply ran out on him. He was tracked down one day in a diner while eating clam chowder.

Fortunately, there are very, very few burglars like J.G. But even he could have been caught in exactly the same way the amateur burglar who sees you leaving can be caught. The best burglary prevention and general crime prevention measure known to man is: people. Specifically, your neighbors.

Whether you live in a single or duplex dwelling, or an apartment house with four, six, eight, or more units, one thing you can count on: your neighbors want to be safe. Just about everyone realizes that they're not as safe today as they were a few years ago, but few people know what to do about it. You've already learned some things and, shortly, you'll learn a lot more.

Right now, you probably know more about crime prevention than your neighbors. They may not have taken the time to find out, but you have. And chances are they'd like you to tell them.

The thing is, you may not know your neighbors, not all of them anyway. And you may not like some of them. But when you help someone and someone helps you, in short order you get to know and like them and they get to know and like you.

Even if you don't want to become friends with your neighbors, please understand that they can help you. And they can also hurt you.

Let's start with how neighbors can hurt you. If they see some suspicious actions by strangers near your home but don't call the police, they're hurting you. Not intentionally, but they are hurting you. The excuse is "We don't want to get involved." The point is they're not very interested in you. If, for example, your neighbor's son or daughter lived in your home and strange men in a parked car were watching it, you'd better believe the neighbors would investigate or call the police or at least make sure the men in the car knew they were being watched.

Neighbors can also hurt you by telling strangers confidential information about you. Sometimes neighbors don't even realize that the private facts they are mentioning are confidential. But when a neighbor tells a stranger who lives where, how many people are in the home, when they are apt to be out, and when they are usually home alone, that information can get around.

On the other hand, neighbors can help you. They are near you and can answer a call for help. They can also hear glass breaking, a dog barking, or sounds of a struggle. And when you leave on an errand, your neighbors can be keeping an eye on your home.

Raymond was a professional burglar, the kind who would find a likely neighborhood, sit in his car, and wait for someone to leave. He wouldn't "case *a* joint," he'd keep his eyes on several homes in the neighborhood. And, incidentally, he'd never say he was "casing a joint." He calls it "waiting in the car and looking." It didn't matter to him whether it was day or night, just that someone leave the home and drive or walk away. Then he'd move in.

This lithe, athletic man of about twenty-two told me how he used to operate:

> [How do you know someone hasn't remained at home when others leave?] I don't know. Sometimes you can tell, sometimes you can't. I ring the bell to make sure.
>
> [If a home has a burglar-alarm system or a big dog or is locked up tight, will that matter?] Yeah. I'd probably go back to the car and wait for someone to leave another home.
>
> [What about neighbors? Maybe they know the people are going out and are watching their home.] Could be. I look around the neighborhood, you know. See if I can see anyone looking.
>
> [And if neighbors are looking?] I move on.
>
> [To a different neighborhood?] Sure. But it doesn't happen much. People go about their own lives.

It happens more than Raymond wanted to discuss. In fact, he was caught and sent to prison because a neighbor saw him near a home, called the police, and the police caught Raymond on his way out.

And please note that just the fact that neighbors kept a lookout on each other's homes was enough to cause him to drive on.

Several cities have programs that encourage citizens to keep an eye on their own neighborhoods. In Philadelphia, the program is called "Operation Town Watch." In Los Angeles, it's called "Neighborhood Watch." These programs are too new to have scientifically valid figures of their effectiveness, though unofficial opinions are that these programs of citizen involvement cannot help but reduce burglaries.

Neighbors who look out for each other not only deter crime, they help the police catch burglars, car thieves, and, occasionally, child molesters and rapists. Most of the time, however, the suspect's actions are only slightly suspicious or not suspicious at all. Even the unsophisticated burglar will try to fit into the area by looking like one of the neighborhood kids. Because their suspicions are only slightly aroused, people are reluctant to call the police.

People, probably yourself included, are reluctant to call the police for another reason: you don't want to bother them. "It's probably nothing and I'd feel like a fool if they came out here for no reason." Just about everyone thinks that way, much to the displeasure of most chiefs of police. Here's what a top Chicago official has to say: "We want you to know that we're glad to send help *before* trouble occurs—please call even though you may not be sure whether it's serious."

A third reason you may not want to call the police is that you don't want to get involved. Perhaps you do care about your neighborhood and your neighbors, but you don't want to get involved with the police. Police departments know this and many have special, confidential numbers that enable you to report suspicious persons or criminal activities anonymously. Use their confidential number if you don't want to give your name. And if they don't have a confidential number, you can call the regular number, give the information, and withhold your name.

Here is a list of some activities to report to the police. This list is for you and your neighbors:

> Be suspicious of that man you have never seen before. Candy sellers, teen-agers selling subscriptions, a salesman, any stranger may use an unanswered doorbell as the opportunity to enter an unsecured home.
>
> That person, young or old, "taking a short cut" through your backyard may have broken into your neighbor's home.
>
> Any stranger entering your neighbor's home when it is unoccupied, or a person carrying household goods, appliances, or so forth from your neighbor's home.
>
> A scream heard anywhere.
>
> Persons offering merchandise at ridiculous prices.

The sound of breaking glass or loud explosive noises.

Broken or open doors or windows.

Strangers or strange cars in your neighborhood, school area, or park.

Anyone loitering in a parked car or in a secluded area.

Persons parking one car and traveling off in another.

Persons walking down the street looking into parked cars.

A fight or any display of weapons such as guns, knives, or clubs.

Any injured person you observe.

And most important, *never* assume that someone else has called the police. *You* call.

Most of the items on this list are courtesy of the Dallas Police Department, which adds that you should be sure to report:

1. Location and type of incident.
2. Number of persons involved or injuries if any.
3. Description of suspects, age, height, weight, dress, complexion, scars, tattoos, jewelry worn by persons, or mannerisms.
4. License number of car involved, also the make, the color, the year, and the direction in which the car may be traveling.

Wouldn't you feel safer if you knew that your neighbors had this information and would act upon it? All you have to do is show it to them or talk to them about it and they may cooperate with you. Maybe you'll make some new friends, maybe not. But once you know your neighbors and their cars by sight and have agreed to look out for each other, your neighborhood will be safer. And so will you.

The illustration on the following page will help you get started. Fill in the numbers of your police and fire departments, then fill in your neighbors' names and phone numbers. The Seattle Crime Prevention Advisory Commission recommends it to you.

Hopefully, you already know and trust a few of your neighbors, and have given one a spare key to your house or apartment. If not, maybe your new contact with the same or other neighbors will introduce you to someone you can trust with your key.

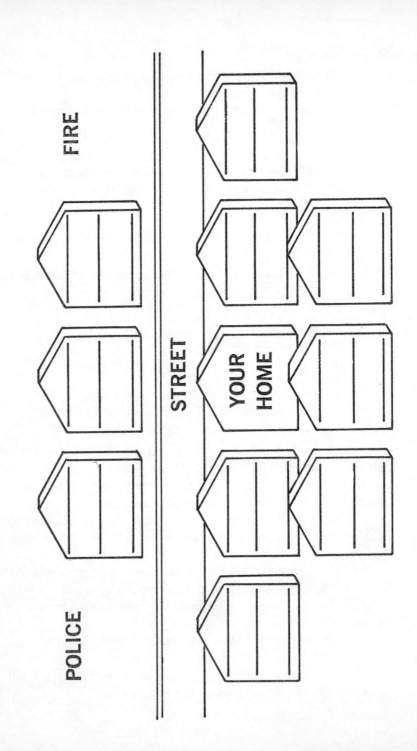

But what happens if you can't trust any of your neighbors?

Raymond, the athletic burglar, complained to me of a problem he had. During the time he was burglarizing homes, he was angry because *he* was getting burglarized! Not only could he never trust his neighbors to watch his place, he was pretty sure his neighbors were burglarizing him.

So he moved. He was still in a bad neighborhood so he moved again because he kept getting burglarized. Now that he's going straight and living in still a different neighborhood, he's not taking chances. "I never keep money in my apartment and I keep my things hidden from view."

There are many suggestions for people who live in good or bad neighborhoods. If your neighbors are trustworthy, there's still no reason to tempt them or their youngsters, or gardeners, painters, roofers, or other help that may work around the home. Money, jewelry, watches, cameras, small antiques, portable electronic equipment like cassette recorders, adding machines, and typewriters should not be left on window sills, on shelves at or next to windows, nor should they be easily seen through windows. The same goes for stamp, coin, gun, and other valuable collections.

Keep money, stocks, and bonds and as many other valuables as possible in the bank. Says an investigator in Los Angeles, "You'd be surprised how many people still keep money around the house." Use a checking account. People also leave jewelry on window sills when they're washing up, which creates golden opportunities for thefts. (In addition to decreasing the visibility of valuables within your house or apartment, you can beef up your security. Locks and the safety habits that go with them are discussed in the next chapter.)

Sometimes suggestions in this book are going to cause you inconvenience. Sometimes they're going to make you change some dangerous habits. But, in reality, this book can't make you do anything. Only you can. It's your house or apartment, it's your money and jewelry and other possessions. More importantly, it's your well-being and that of your man or children or roommate.

A top official of Dallas says it this way: "A police officer cannot be on your block or your street all the time, therefore you can assist the police by acting as their eyes and ears."

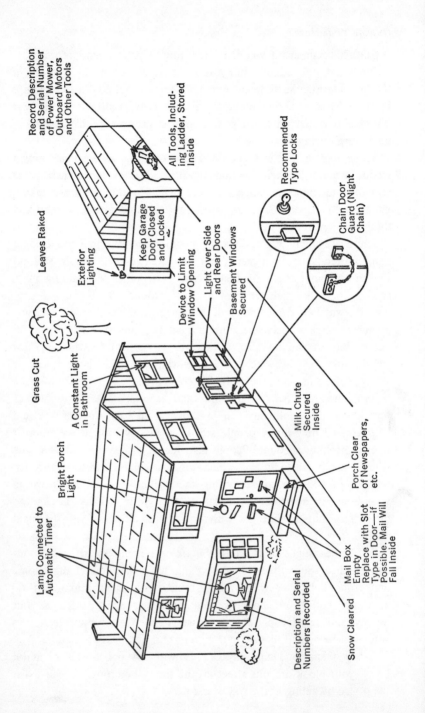

Record Description and Serial Number of Power Mower, Outboard Motors and Other Tools

All Tools, Including Ladder, Stored Inside

Leaves Raked

Keep Garage Door Closed and Locked

Exterior Lighting

Recommended Type Locks

Chain Door Guard (Night Chain)

Device to Limit Window Opening

Light over Side and Rear Doors

Basement Windows Secured

Grass Cut

A Constant Light in Bathroom

Milk Chute Secured Inside

Bright Porch Light

Porch Clear of Newspapers, etc.

Lamp Connected to Automatic Timer

Mail Box Empty Replace with Slot Type in Door—if Possible. Mail Will Fall Inside

Description and Serial Numbers Recorded

Snow Cleared

You can also assist yourself by enlisting the help of your neighbors and by protecting your own home.

Take a moment right now and walk outside your home. You've been introduced to a few burglars, so look at your home the way Bill or Jim would. They are young burglars who dote on opportunities such as open doors or windows. Then try to determine what C.T. or Larry, two hypes, would think. Could they get in and out fast? And then think of Roger and Raymond, two pros. They can get around most security devices, but neither they nor any of the other burglars want to meet up with you. Can you tell if anyone is home right now? Could you tell yesterday just as you were coming home?

The illustration on page 30 will help you make your home safer from the outside and is supplied courtesy of the Detroit Police Department. If your home is easy to get into, you'll learn how to harden the target!

3

Inside Your Home

Inside your home is where you are. Inside your home is also where your loved ones are. Your home has just *got* to be safe.

I've heard some people say, "If someone wants to break into a home bad enough, there's no way to stop him."

There's far *less* truth in that statement than meets the eye. As you already know, burglary is the biggest reason for breaking into homes, and almost all burglars either want to be sure you're not home or that you're fast asleep before they enter.

Burglars and rapists are lazy and cowardly. There are very few cases of their being so motivated that they will take the time and effort to break into a secure home. Time and difficulty are deterrents to crime.

Detroit crime-prevention experts explain the situation this way: "The burglarproof house has not yet been designed. However, it is possible to take some simple precautionary measures which will make the burglar's task as difficult and frustrating as possible. . . . Remember, delay of a potential burglar in gaining entry increases the chances of his being apprehended. Place as many obstacles between him and his goal as possible."

Putting obstacles in his way may deter him and it may also enable a neighbor to spot him while he tries to break in. Interested neighbors plus precautionary measures are the very closest you can come to a burglarproof home.

On the other hand, if you leave your doors open or unlocked, you are making your home insecure. Perhaps you are a fairly careful person. You make sure all the doors are locked when you leave your house or apartment. If so, you are acting to prevent crime.

But what about closing and locking doors when you are inside? A great many people leave doors and windows open, or closed but unlocked, when they or children, mothers, fathers, elderly people, or guests are inside. It's bad enough that a burglar or other illegal intruder may break into your home when no one is there. Surely you don't want any stranger sneaking into your home when you or a loved one is inside, do you?

And that's the main reason for keeping doors and windows closed and locked when you're home: to avoid confrontation with a burglar, rapist, or other potential felon.

Should doors be closed and locked every second of the day? And the same with windows? What about during hot weather? If you don't have air conditioning, you want some of the windows open. What do you do then? Must you also have expensive burglar alarms plus a vicious dog?

You don't want to make your home a fortress. What you do want is a house or apartment that is safe and secure and comfortable. You want to be able to relax, knowing that you and those close to you don't have to worry or be afraid of strangers breaking in.

Some people don't want to think about shutting and locking doors, about the best locks to have, about securing windows. They'd rather keep things "wide open." For them, locking doors and windows means that they can't relax.

According to the FBI, 18 per cent of all burglaries involve no forced entry. There is no breakdown on the number of aggravated assaults, rapes, and murders as to where they took place and if entry into a home was forced or not. But the Los Angeles Police

Department does have some surprising figures on burglary. No forced entry was involved in 60 per cent of burglaries last year. Burglars simply walked or climbed in open or unlocked doors and windows.

Larry, the hype who would never go into a home with lights or a radio on, absolutely never wanted to meet any people. He's a very nervous man, especially when he has illegally entered someone's home. He and his two partners would make every attempt to find out if someone was in a home or not. If not, they'd go in. If so, they'd move on. Many times, however, their appraisal proved incorrect. In the following case, which Larry told me, he was wrong with comical results:

> It was early, about seven in the morning. We were in a working neighborhood where people leave home early and we spotted this one house. Looked like no one was home but I rang the front bell just in case. No one answered.

> We went around the back. The back door wasn't locked so we looked around and went in.

> One guy watched the street in case someone came home. My other partner and I went through the bedroom and the study. We took money and maybe jewelry like watches.

> As we were coming out of the bedroom, suddenly we hear a toilet flush and out of the bathroom comes a woman. Now when I get in a house, my heart is going a thousand times a minute. And that's when the house is empty.

> So when we saw her, we bolted for that back door so fast, we tore it half off its hinges. We started racing down the street as fast as we could. But this woman ran out of the house yelling, "Burglars, burglars."

> Man, were we scared. We kept running. People started coming out of homes, hearing this woman yelling, seeing what was wrong. The people were in bathrobes and hair curlers and the woman kept yelling, "Help, burglars, burglars!"

> We were running and looking over our shoulders until we realized something: we were running down a dead-end street!

> Like I told you, we were scared. But the only thing to do was to turn around and run back. So we turned around and started racing up the street.

> There were all these people on the lawns and looking out

windows and this crazy woman yelling, "Help, help." But as we started running back up the street, she got hysterical. She started yelling, "They're coming back. Here they come again!"

Larry and his comrades made it to their car and drove off. When the police were finally called, the burglars were nowhere to be seen.

In Larry's story, I hope you noticed that the back door had not been locked. And let's be honest. Larry and his partners didn't hit this house because the back door was unlocked. That may be the case with young burglars, but Larry was a pro. He could probably have gotten into this house even if the door had been locked.

Probably, but by no means definitely. It depends on the lock, the delay it would cause, the noise he might have had to make, and the chance that a neighbor might see him. Burglars have neither the time to waste on a secure home nor, usually, the desire to get into any particular home. Larry, and just about every other burglar, wants to get in and out fast.

Any way you look at it, leaving doors and windows open or shutting them but leaving them unlocked is asking for trouble. Locked screen doors and locked window screens are no help either, since they can so easily be cut. Although that woman was untouched by Larry and his partners, you'd better believe she was frightened.

Secure your doors and windows. Have tough locks and use them. If you're going to leave doors and windows open, sooner or later someone will come in. Doors and windows go together; secure them and your home will be safer.

DOORS

Houses and apartments have front doors, back doors, side doors, porch doors, double doors, sliding doors, bulkhead doors, basement doors, and cellar doors. The doors are made of wood (solid or hollow or paneled) or wood with glass panels (such as kitchen doors) or metal. I know one man whose large home has nine exterior doors, and you know that a burglar or other offender will choose the easiest way to break in. If the front door is secured, he'll head for the back or side door.

All exterior doors should be secure. But since a lock is only as strong as the door it's on, your doors are your first line of defense.

Solid wood or metal doors are obviously the strongest. Hollow and paneled doors can be sawed or broken through without much difficulty. While a burglar won't sit outside your front door sawing away in broad daylight, he might spend a little time on a secluded side door. Should the need exist, it is possible to reinforce hollow or paneled doors by adding a piece of sheet steel or plywood to the inside and/or the outside. Attach the steel or plywood with nonretractable screws and be sure the existing hinges can take the added weight.

Wooden doors with glass panels are common in kitchens and porches, presenting an easy entrance to an intruder. He can simply tape a glass panel, then break it, put a gloved hand through, and open the door from the inside. Hardware and building-supply stores have reinforced glass or strong transparent plastic that can replace the fragile glass in these doors. Or you can have a double-cylinder lock installed (though this can cause problems, so see the discussion on locks below).

Sliding-glass doors are more often neglected than glass-paneled doors. The standard locks on many sliding-glass doors are not strong, and people very seldom have reinforced glass in these doors. You need added security here. Buy a strong wooden dowel that is about an inch and a half in diameter and about an inch shorter than the length of one sliding door, then slip the dowel in the door's channel. If a broom handle meets these measurements, use it instead. Better yet, have a downward-sloping hole drilled through the top and bottom corners of the moving door's frame and halfway through the other door's frame. Then slip a metal pin through the hole and your sliding door won't slide. If you want the door to be open an inch or two, drill more holes on the stationary door an inch or two from the first. Although these dowels and pins are inexpensive, they are not as effective as locks. For example, you can't use dowels and pins to secure the door from the outside when you leave. (Some inexpensive and some expensive sliding-door locks are presented later in this chapter.)

Various parts of the door are fundamental to your control over who comes into your house and who stays out. The hinges, for example, should be on the inside. If they're on the outside, the pins can be removed and the door taken off. Check your exterior doors, and if the hinges are on the outside you need to have non-removable pins installed.

And while you're checking your door, take a close look at the doorjamb and the fit of the door. The doorjamb and molding should be solid. If they are loose or rotting, they can be pried off, giving the burglar a below-the-belt shot at the exposed lock. You want as little space as possible between the door and the jamb. The greater the clearance, the greater the ease in attacking the lock. Some locks have face plates that, when properly angled, can reduce the space between the door and jamb. More simply, a row of nails or strips of metal in the area of the latch can solve this problem.

Let's pause just a second. I know that many women and men are turned off by technical discussions of things like doors and doorjambs and locks. I've eliminated all but the most important points and simplified these as much as possible. What's here is vital. For an expert and thorough view of your doors, contact a licensed locksmith. Your police department might have men specially trained to make inspections of private residences.

LOCKS

All doors, interior and exterior, with locks have spring-latch locks. These spring latches automatically "lock" when you close the door. But for exterior doors, you need dead-bolt locks that are locked by hand. Just about any amateur can disengage a spring-latch lock, but a dead bolt will slow down even the best of the pros.

Doors come equipped with either key-in-the-knob locks (the most popular and least secure kind) or mortise locks. Both of these locks work with a doorknob or door handle and are termed "primary locks." The fact that the key goes right in the knob of the former enables a burglar who's not afraid of making noise to hammer away at the knob, break it off, and open the door. That, however, is the least of the problems with the key-in-the-knob lock.

More fundamental is the small extension of the bolt. Seldom

will the bolt of this spring-latch lock extend more than a quarter or a half an inch into the jamb. In addition, because this spring-latch lock is beveled in order to close automatically, it can be opened almost as easily by inserting a thin credit card or a piece of Celluloid between the latch and the strike. (This is called loiding a lock.)

Most important, compare your key-in-the-knob locks with the following illustration. If your lock doesn't have a trigger bolt, it is *not* providing security. The trigger bolt depresses when the door is closed and keeps the latch from being pushed back. If you have no trigger bolt, you have trouble.

KEY-IN-THE-KNOB LOCK

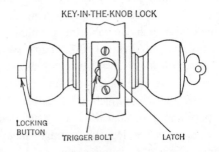

LOCKING
BUTTON
TRIGGER BOLT   LATCH

You can leave a door with a key-in-the-knob lock or a mortise lock "on the latch" and thereby leave yourself no security. Properly used, however, mortise locks are more secure than key-in-the-knob locks because the mortise has a spring-latch lock *and* a horizontal dead-bolt lock. The cylinder of the mortise lock (the area where you insert the key) is not located in a knob or handle but is enclosed in metal inside the door. The spring latch of the mortise lock may be just as short and ineffective as the spring latch of the key-in-the-knob lock. The main benefit of the mortise lock is the dead bolt, if it's an inch long. But if the dead bolt doesn't extend much more than the spring latch, it's just more of the same inadequate protection.

A good-looking, strong mortise lock will retail for anywhere from $35 to $75. Don't spend this money, however, if the dead bolt doesn't extend one inch or if you won't bother to use it.

The setscrews you see in the illustration of the mortise lock hold

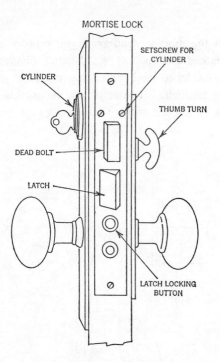

MORTISE LOCK

SETSCREW FOR CYLINDER

CYLINDER

THUMB TURN

DEAD BOLT

LATCH

LATCH LOCKING BUTTON

the cylinder in place. Weiser, Arrow, Yale, Abloy, and others manufacture mortise locks with protective metal plates covering these setscrews. If the mortise lock on your door doesn't have this metal plate, cover the setscrews with some putty or nail polish. That way a dishonest delivery person may be deterred from rubbing through the coating, loosening the screws, and returning later to burglarize the home.

Auxiliary locks, which are added to the primary locks, are available in many varieties. If your front door has a solid mortise lock with a one-inch dead bolt, you won't need an auxiliary lock on that door. But what about the others?

You *need* a vertical or horizontal dead-bolt lock on every exterior door in your house or apartment. The New York Police Department says, "Use a double lock or dead bolt at all times. . . . The double lock or dead bolt requires the use of your key to turn the bolt when you are leaving, and a turn of the bolt when you are inside." You can't be safe only by letting the spring-latch lock engage itself. You must double lock your door with a dead bolt.

Just as with the mortise dead bolt, you want a horizontal dead-bolt lock to extend one inch. The following illustration also shows a free-turning hardened-steel insert that makes it impossible for a burglar to saw through. The rim of the cylinder is beveled, which makes it hard to tamper with. These locks cost between $10 and $20.

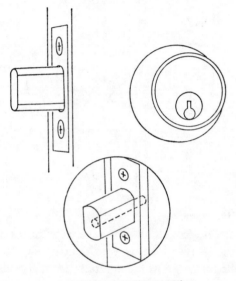

HORIZONTAL DEAD BOLT LOCK

Many licensed locksmiths and police experts prefer the vertical dead bolt to all other auxiliary locks. With Segal, or "jimmy-proof" locks, the vertical dead bolt is secured to its mating plate much as a door hinge is secured by its pin. The least expensive models of this lock retail for about $7.00 while locks offering longer life can cost over $20. Segal and Yale make excellent vertical dead-bolt locks, as do some others. The least expensive models, however, are not top quality. With all makes of this lock, be sure to install carefully so that the screws fit solidly into a strong doorjamb and door and the two pieces mate tightly.

Double-cylinder locks are for use in all types of doors, especially those with some glass in them. While most locks have a cylinder on

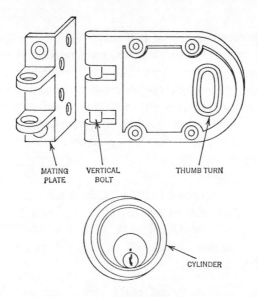

MATING PLATE   VERTICAL BOLT   THUMB TURN

CYLINDER

VERTICAL DEAD BOLT LOCK

the outside (you insert the key in the cylinder and unlock the door) and a thumb turn on the inside, double-cylinder locks have a cylinder on the outside and a second cylinder on the inside. When you double lock the door while you're inside, you need a key to get out.

The advantage of a double-cylinder lock is that a burglar also needs a key to get in or out. These locks are particularly useful on glass-paneled doors because if a person breaks the glass and sticks his hand inside the door, he will still need a key to unlock it. Similarly, if a burglar enters through a window and all the door locks in the home are double-cylinder, he can't exit through a door carrying large objects. He will have to exit through the window.

But double-cylinder locks have some big disadvantages for children and guests. These people may not have keys to the lock, they may not know where the keys are kept, and they may not even be able to reach the lock. So if there's a fire or other emergency, they will be unable to exit by a door that has a double-cylinder lock.

Detective Larry Carr of New York has the following suggestions regarding this lock: "Don't leave a key in the lock when you're inside and don't hang a key near the lock if the key will be visible. These actions defeat the purpose of the lock. Instead, have two auxiliary locks, a single-cylinder dead bolt and a double-cylinder dead bolt. Use the double-cylinder lock only when you're *not* at home."

When you leave your home and when you enter it, the spring latch on the primary lock (key-in-the-knob or mortise) will engage. "One of the best security habits to develop," says Sergeant Lee Kirkwood of Los Angeles, "is to double lock your door." Close and lock it with the primary lock, then turn your dead-bolt lock so you have solid security.

Carlos is a professional burglar. In the following case history, he was so strongly motivated that he might even have been able to get past a door with a dead bolt. The back door of this home didn't have one so he was inside with no difficulty and went about his crime with ribald results:

> This loan shark had really soaked me with interest so I figured I'd do something about it. He wasn't charging, you know, fair interest or anything so I decided *he* ought to pay it, not me.
>
> I followed him home one night. It was about ten o'clock when he went in the door. I sat in my car and smoked cigarettes for almost three hours. It was about one in the morning, his house was quiet, no lights had been on for over an hour. Now was my time.
>
> The back door had a lock that my jackknife took care of in a minute and I was in the kitchen. Then I saw something. Staring me right in the face was this tiny, hairless Mexican Chihuahua.
>
> I don't like dogs, I really don't. Never did. And this little runt was about to start barking. So I knelt down real quick and talked to him, talked to him very quietly. "Nice doggy" sort of crap, you know. He was awful nervous and ready to wake up everybody so I shot out a hand and grabbed his body, pulled him to me, and muzzled him with my other hand. Then I ran over to the refrigerator and threw him in.
>
> I took a minute, then tiptoed down the hallway and toward the stairs. I just knew a man like that wouldn't have money in a safe or anything. He'd keep it right near him. That's what my instincts told me. And I was right.

Up the stairs I went. I was looking at all the paintings and antiques the guy collected. Man, he was really raking it in. But as I was walking up the stairs, I began to hear a noise, a creaking sort of noise. I got to the top of the stairs and crouched down to find out where the hell the noise was coming from. I look around and then I see this guy making it with his old lady in the bedroom.

It's about one in the morning and I'm taking all this trouble and there's the bastard balling his wife. On my time!

Well, you know I'm not going to turn around and leave. There's money in that bedroom and I'm going to get it. So I move to the bedroom—all the time there's this creaking sound, sort of nerve-wracking—and over on the far side of bed, over a chair, are his pants with a bulge in the pocket. His wallet.

I hate to say it but on my hands and knees I crawl across the room, past the creaking bed, to that chair. I get the pants and that thick, beautiful wallet, stuff the money in my pants, and start back.

All the time I hear this creaking, creaking. You know, it's getting to me. So I'm crawling past the bed and there's the bastard's bare ass going up and down. But as I move past the bed, I see something underneath. A wooden slat is on the floor. I look over at the guy's bare ass, I look back at the wooden slat, and I know I've just gotta do it.

I reach under the bed, grab the slat, move over right behind the guy and stand up. Just as his ass comes up in the air, I give a yell and let him have it with the slat. He hollers as he goes down, his old lady screams, and I run out.

Then down the stairs, through the hallway, into the kitchen and to the refrigerator. I yank out the dog. He stands on the floor, shivering all over. Then I run out the back door and I'm laughing so hard I pee in my pants.

There is a serious point to Carlos' story. When an offender is strongly motivated, he'll take risks that he wouldn't otherwise take. His fear of being caught will be a little less important than his desire to commit a particular crime. There are also some burglars and other felons who aren't too afraid of being caught. I have no idea how many of these men there are. But because they are depressed and see no other way than a life of crime, because they feel they can outwit the private citizen and the police, because they feel that they will only get a light sentence or no sentence at all, because they may actually want to go back to prison, there are some criminals who are not afraid of being caught.

OTHER LOCKS, OTHER HARDWARE

You can find some sort of home-security device in just about any store you go into. Before you buy any lock, think through what you expect it to do and be very sure it can do that before you put down your money.

Most door chains, for example, will not keep a strong man out. The nails are often too short and the metal is usually too thin. Door chains can also be easily disengaged if they are not installed very carefully. But door chains are probably the most popular auxiliary device there is, mainly because they're inexpensive. So if you want to buy one or already have one on the door, make sure that the screws are long and that the metal is sturdy. Also make sure that the molding you'll screw it into is strong enough to take the force of an adult man trying to get in. Chances are that either the molding or the metal bracket will give, even if it is one of the locking door chains.

Be sure to leave no more than an inch for the door to open when the chain is attached. You don't want an unwelcome hand coming through. Unfortunately, door chains are used as "interviewers." They are seldom adequate as auxiliary locks, and when the primary lock is disengaged and only the door chain is on, you have too little protection. The door is open about an inch so you can see who's on the other side, but if that person wants to get in he has only to break through that little chain.

Far better than door chains used as interviewers are interviewers themselves. They include a small panel of glass or a small hole in the door that is closed by a piece of metal or glass. Also called peepholes, interviewers are inexpensive. Through-the-door viewers are more costly, look like miniature telescopes, and provide a wide-angle view of the caller. These tube-like devices also have a slipcover for the inside that prevents people from looking in at you. To look out, you move the cover aside.

Interviewing grills, look-and-talk devices, and most other equipment for eye-level sighting of a caller are preferable to door chains that are used as interviewers. Many cities, including New York, make it a law that all apartment doors have interviewers.

My wife has a very good use for a door chain. Since our little boy can reach and unlock our primary and auxiliary locks, my wife put a door chain at her eye level, using it not to keep others out but to keep our son in.

Double doors can also cause problems that are solved by special locks. A tiny bolt is most often found on double doors to keep the second door stationary. A thick, commercial-type half-inch bolt is much better protection against the second door being kicked in. Cane bolts one half inch in diameter and twelve inches high installed at the top and bottom are even more effective. The second door also acts as the doorjamb for the active door so make sure a dead bolt extends well into the stationary door.

Thick barrel-bolt locks and their more modern equivalents (sometimes called door bolts) are adequate for placement on the interior side of attic and cellar doors and bulkheads to deter access into the main rooms of a house. Only the very strongest of these locks, however, are capable of giving security to exterior doors and all have the disadvantage that they cannot be locked from the outside.

Special locks for sliding-glass doors include the Charley Bar, made by Schlage, which is similar to but much better than a broom handle in the door channel. Adams-Rite makes several different keyed locks that are far superior to the average lock in your sliding-glass door. At about $10.00 plus the price of a cylinder, these locks aren't inexpensive but you can secure your door from the inside or the outside and have the peace of mind that your sliding-glass door is just about as strong as your front door. Schlage, P.T.I., and many others make less expensive devices for sliding-glass doors. Most are designed to pin your door in position and some require a padlock.

Just because your sliding-glass door faces the side or the back of your home, don't neglect it. If it's the weakest link in your chain of home security, that's where a burglar will enter.

If you live in a high crime area or want to install super-security locks, there are door braces that reinforce the door with a rod of metal that runs from the door down to a hole in the floor, or the Fox Police Double-bolt Lock that sends extensions of tough metal into the right and the left doorjambs. These models cost between $30 and $90 installed. If you're interested in them, determine whether you want to be able to lock them from both the outside and the inside (some lock only from the outside).

Whatever locks you decide to have on your doors, make sure all your doors are secure. Also if you get carried away and have too many locks installed, you can be in trouble. Some homes in high crime areas have four or more locks on the door. That's not good protection, that's a fire trap! A primary and a good auxiliary lock are all you need to secure your home and be able to get in or out fast in an emergency.

You may be handy with tools or know a great do-it-yourselfer. A licensed locksmith, however, is the best person to advise you on locks and to install them professionally. Many locksmiths will make a security check of your home and not charge if you purchase their locks and services. You can also purchase top-quality locks at most hardware and building-supply stores, though the salespeople are not as highly trained to advise you as are licensed locksmiths.

Good locks cost money. So does professional installation. Most locksmiths charge from the time they leave their shop until they return. Fees across the country vary. But there's no sense in spending good money for poor locks or for faulty installation, or for unlicensed locksmiths who may not be trustworthy. If you must save the extra dollars, compare the quality of different brands of locks, then check the door after it has been installed to make sure it's secure. If there's any play or if it's hard to open or close, you have not spent your money wisely.

KEYS

"There are people who never lock their doors, who don't even know where their door keys are." Those are the words of an investigator who is part of Team 28, a special antiburglary campaign being conducted in Venice, California, and several other cities. Strong doors and secure locks will do you no good if you or others in your home are careless with keys.

The rules for keys are simple. Have all your keys with you or keep those you're not using in a safe place. Separate your home and car keys when you absolutely must leave your car key with an attendant. Never put your name or your address on any key. Never hide any key outside your home, inside or outside your car. Never leave a key in the door of your home or the ignition of your car.

You don't need to replace the locks when you move into a new home (unless the locks are inadequate) but you should have the locks re-keyed. A locksmith can do this quite easily. It's also safer to have the locks re-keyed if you or someone else in the family loses a key or if unreliable domestic help with access to your keys is let go.

If, on the other hand, you leave keys in your coat when you're in a restaurant, or house keys with a parking-lot attendant when you're shopping, a person can quickly make an impression of your key in soap or clay then have a key made that fits your lock.

STRANGERS AT THE DOOR

Some offenders don't bash down doors or jimmy locks or use duplicate keys to steal into your home. Instead, people let them in. Sometimes the callers will be burglars or accomplices who will look around the home, perhaps tamper with a latch, and return later. Other times they are rapists who will attack as soon as they get in.

None of these people will look like criminals. The intruder may wear a business suit or a service uniform of the electric, gas, telephone, or some other company. He may be a nice-looking schoolboy or a man dressed up like a woman. I have seen case histories of burglars and rapists dressed all these ways; there was even the case of two women who claimed car trouble and murdered an elderly lady who let them in to use her phone.

While you may have read similar stories in the newspaper, there is a variation that is not so widely known. Instead of asking to come into your home, the caller tries to get you to come out. One woman in her forties told the following to the police:

> A neatly dressed man knocked at my door in the middle of the afternoon. I left the chain on the door and opened it to look out. He wore a business suit but seemed upset about something. "Yes?" I asked.
>
> "Someone's just hit your car," he said.
>
> "Oh, no," I said. "Is it bad?"
>
> "No," he responded, "not too bad but you'd better take a look."
>
> I agreed with him, closed the door to unlatch the chain, and opened the door to start out. He pushed right into the house, slammed the door, and ripped my dress down the front.

"There are so many rapes of this sort," says Sergeant Bud Carr of Los Angeles, who investigates sex crimes against women and children. "*All* of them could be prevented if women were simply more cautious about opening their doors to strangers."

No matter how familiar the uniform a caller is wearing or how clean-cut he looks, if you don't know the man at the door, he's a stranger. Always be suspicious of *unscheduled* visits by building inspectors, census takers, telephone repairmen, plumbers, termite inspectors, and others. If you have doubts about a person, ask to be given some identification. He can slip it under the door and you can call the organization he claims to work for. Every legitimate caller will hand you his identification, from police to reputable salesmen to tax assessors. These people have nothing to hide.

If someone comes to your door seeking to use your phone, you can be friendly and safe by asking them to remain outside while you make the call for them. Sergeant Bud Carr concludes, "Never let total strangers in either for good or for trivial reasons. And never let strangers trick you into unlocking your doors."

Since a person may come to any of your exterior doors, don't be cautious only at the front door. Every outside door provides an entrance to your home. If there's a caller and you don't want to answer the door, don't. Or if you do but you're alone, pretend a man is with you and say, "That's all right, honey, I'll get it."

WINDOWS

Every window on the first or second story provides an entrance to your house. Although burglars very seldom break a window for fear the noise will attract attention, windows with only the standard flimsy latches will not keep an intruder out. All windows need strong, usually keyless, locks that keep them closed or devices that secure them open a little in set positions.

Basement windows of many houses are very often completely neglected. Unless someone is working in the basement at the time, these windows should always be kept shut and locked and covered. You can buy strong locks for these windows, though in some homes basement windows do have locks capable of minimum security. And either cover these windows with cloth or paint them from the inside.

Double-hung windows are very common in houses and apartments and their locks are almost always inadequate. You can buy keyed and unkeyed locks for these windows or you can save some money. If you never use a window, nail or screw it shut. If you do use it, drill a downward sloping hole into the top of the bottom window and part way through the bottom of the top window. When the window is shut, it can be locked by inserting a nail or a pin. If you want it open, drill two more downward sloping holes an inch or, at

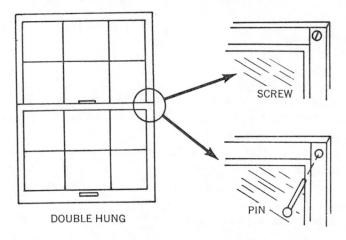

DOUBLE HUNG   SCREW   PIN

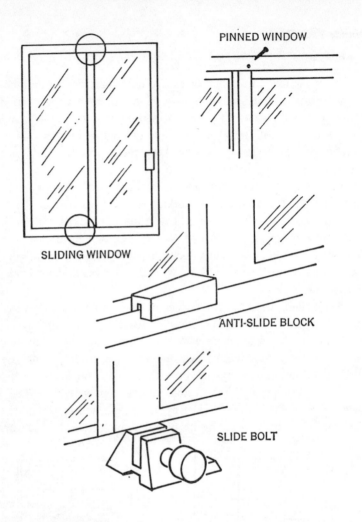

PINNED WINDOW

SLIDING WINDOW

ANTI-SLIDE BLOCK

SLIDE BOLT

most, two inches from the bottom of the top window. Drill these holes only part way through the top window so that the pin or nail can't be pulled out from the outside.

Locking a window in a ventilating position, however, provides less security because it facilitates prying. If it's hot and you have no air conditioning, rely as much as possible on fans, not open (even secured) windows.

Sliding-glass windows can be secured in ways similar to sliding-glass doors. As with the doors, you want to keep these windows from sliding or being lifted up and out of the channel. Since most burglars don't want to make the noise necessary to break glass on this or other windows, pin the windows or buy inexpensive anti-slide blocks or slide bolts.

Louver windows are bad security risks. If possible, remove and replace them with solid glass double-hung or casement windows. Otherwise, consider installing a grille or grate outside louver windows.

But be careful with wrought-iron or steel grilles and grates or windows with keyed locks. Every bedroom should have one window available as a fire exit. At night, the bedroom window may be the quickest means of escape. *Always* have only a strong *un*keyed lock with no other devices (no pins, nails, wedges, locks, grilles, or grates) on one window in each bedroom. And keep that window locked.

Casement windows are the simplest to secure. Make sure the latch works properly and that the crank has no excess play. If it does, replace the worn handle. As with other windows, it's safest to have them closed:

> Mrs. Sadie Morrison was awakened at 2 A.M. on a recent Friday by a strange noise outside her fourth-story apartment window. She had retired four hours earlier, leaving her casement windows open a little. These windows stand over a narrow ledge.
>
> Mrs. Morrison crept to her windows and cranked them open. Then she heard a loud scream.
>
> She looked down and later told the police she could barely see the form of a man lying on the ground. After a moment, the man limped off.
>
> The burglar had made his way going the ledge outside Mrs. Morrison's apartment and was apparently holding onto her windows when she cranked them open.

Your window coverings (curtains, drapes, shades, or blinds) are also crime-prevention devices for they keep outsiders from seeing what's inside. Be particularly careful about the coverings in your bedroom and other rooms where women or girls are undressing or in night clothes. Just an inch or two of uncovered window can give a peeping tom all the view he needs.

ALARMS

There are some dead-bolt locks that also have alarms. Stanley, 3M, and others manufacture these combination locks and alarms that are excellent for doors, are easy to install, have no wires because they run on batteries, and sound the alarm when there's any attempt at forced entry. Prices run from $60 to $100 per unit.

While the purpose of locks is to *prevent* illegal entry, the primary purpose of alarms (excepting the lock plus alarm) is to *detect* housebreaking. Once the alarm unit or system detects an apparent emergency, a noise (bell, siren, or horn) is triggered or lights are turned on or blinked on and off. Although homes can have silent alarms that contact a central station, it is much better to have a local alarm that can alert the occupants and neighbors plus scare off an offender. Local alarms can also send a signal to a central station.

As good as many alarms are, they never are a substitute for strong locks on doors, secure windows, and consistent security habits in using those doors and windows and their keys.

Alarms do, however, give an extra level of security against crime so you might want to consider the many types of units or entire systems that are available. Once again, equipment is not going to be a sole answer to any problem: alarms that sound in the home need neighbors to respond and call for help or come over to assist you. If you decide to install some sort of local alarm, let your neighbors know and ask for their cooperation in an emergency.

Let's start with a quick rundown of the different types of individual alarm units available. The combination lock and alarm has been mentioned and is a fine deterrent, though it in no way protects your windows.

The least expensive alarms fit in the palm of your hand. You can keep one by your bed (or carry it with you when you're outside) and, in event of an emergency, pull a pin and the battery-operated alarm rings (Full alarm systems have similar but more sophisticated panic buttons.)

Many alarm units are tripped by a contact. One small device that sells for about $12 can be placed behind a door or on a window sill. If it's tilted, it emits a piercing sound. There are other battery-operated units designed to be mounted on doors or door frames. These can be set to sound an alarm whether you're in or out by turning them on with a key. Some alarms are in the form of mats, slipping under rugs or carpets near a door and making a noise when stepped on. There are contact alarms for windows and screens that go off when the window or screen is tampered with.

While the contact alarm is activated when something causes the contact to be broken, a second type of unit covers a certain space. These are movement units and employ either ultrasonic waves, photoelectric devices, infrared light, or nondirectional radar. These various alarms are self-contained units that plug into a wall. Some have optional batteries that will run the system in a power blackout or in the event a burglar enters and unplugs the alarm before it sounds. (Most units have a time delay that allows the occupant to enter the room and deactive the equipment to prevent a false alarm.)

Movement units send out light or sound and raise an alarm when motion interrupts the signal or wave. The motion may be caused by a burglar, or by a child, pet, or unaware guest. Also, the sound waves can, if not properly adjusted, upset your pet or even give some members of your family headaches.

All but the most powerful of the movement units, and every one of the contact units, are good only in one area. If you want to protect other areas of your home, you'll need more units. But before you buy several units, realize that your costs will approach that of a burglar-alarm system.

Burglar-alarm systems often start at about $400 and include some components of interior and perimeter protection. Depending upon what you need, these systems can also include fire alarms and can run up to $25,000. So, first, let's discuss the needs of people who most often purchase (or lease) alarm systems.

If your house is isolated, or out of any neighbor's view; if you have many valuable items (such as expensive stamp, coin, or other collections, fine art, costly jewelry); if many burglaries are occurring in your area; if you live alone or are left alone often and fear the danger of forced entry, then you may very well need a burglar-alarm system.

The California Council on Criminal Justice recommends that any alarm system include:

1. A battery fail-safe back-up.
2. Fire-sensing capability.
3. Read-out ability to check the working of the system.
4. A horn-sounding device installed in the attic through a vent.

When an alarm is designed to contact a central station in the event of a burglary or fire, this central station can contact the police or fire department and can also send out its own security force. In some areas you are allowed to have alarm systems wired directly into police and fire departments. Similarly, alarm systems rigged to telephones that automatically contact the police or fire department with a recorded message (called automatic dialers) are allowed in some parts of the country. Both the direct and automatic contact systems are losing favor or are not permissible in many places because of the great number of false alarms.

Before you buy any alarm units or systems, you will want to have experts give objective comments about the best use for your home. Some of the alarm salesmen may be experts (and some may not) but don't count on them to be objective. Their job is to sell. Start with your insurance man, who might have some recommendations and some good news on insurance reductions for certain equipment. Many police departments will also suggest types of units or systems that they find preferable. Many licensed locksmiths can advise you and also install systems (though they probably won't be able to hook your system into a central station).

It is always best to check several stores or several alarm systems before buying anything. Many shoddy companies are producing inferior equipment so never be pressured into deciding. Before buying any alarm unit, know whether you want it to work on contact or on movement (the contact unit usually detects the intruder before he enters while the movement unit detects him when he's in your home). It is always better to purchase a unit that is UL approved, though some new and fine products may be on the market before they've had time for Underwriter's Laboratories to test them.

A.D.T. and Morse are two national, reputable alarm-systems companies that do not engage in high-pressure tactics. My information is that both will give a fairly objective appraisal of your needs. Other firms in your area might be just as good. Check with friends, the Better Business Bureau, or a list of customers furnished by the alarm company.

If a list of customers isn't available, maybe the company hasn't been around long enough for you to know if they are reliable and if they will be there when you need service. Always check with two or three companies to compare their appraisals of the equipment you'll need, the charge for the equipment, its installation, and subsequent service fees. You may also want to learn the costs of leasing alarm systems.

For those who are good with tools, there is money to be saved by doing-it-yourself. These systems are available in kits from radio-parts and hardware stores and by mail, and cost from about $50 to over $250. Despite the money-back guarantees of many mail-order kits, it's better to examine the merchandise beforehand so that you can compare several brands. Therefore I suggest you stick to examining alarm kits in stores. And whether you, your husband, or your friend install the system, make sure it's done very carefully. False security is worse than no security.

GUNS

If you or a member of your family thinks a gun is a good source of protection, you're not alone. Millions of Americans feel this way. Some are content to have their guns locked away in one place, their bullets locked away in another. But others want their guns loaded and near them for protection.

Oakland Chief of Police C. R. Gain has some thoughts on guns that you might want to consider:

> As Chief of Police of Oakland, I have had considerable cause to carefully examine both the nature and the sources of the threat to personal safety that exists in urban America today. My examination has inexorably drawn me to the conclusion that ownership of handguns is, at best, a futile step

and, at worst, an immediate hazard to the very people who seek to protect themselves.

Handguns are a primary source of home accidents. They serve as the major device of domestic homicide and as such represent a far greater threat to human safety than "crime in the streets."

The ownership of handguns is such an emotional issue to some people that it's impossible to talk with them about it. Most of the time a man wants to have a gun to protect himself and his family against a burglar or rapist. Very often, racial fears are also involved.

Views like those of Chief Gain are seldom considered (his further thoughts on guns are found in Chapter 13). In addition, not enough people know about the thoughts of people on the other side of the law. People like a man I call Van. Short, thin, balding, he's somewhere in his thirties, has a pair of darting eyes, a jutting nose, and a mouth that is quick to curl into a smile. He has been a heroin addict, a burglar, a car thief, and a robber. There's no official record of it, but he boasted to me that he's also been a rapist and child molester.

Neither women, money, or heroin have been Van's first love, though. He loves something else:

> Guns. Oh, guns. You hold that black, shiny strong thing in your hands. You feel it. It's like a woman, better than a woman, better than the most beautiful woman. A gun. Oh, I like guns. I *really* like guns.
>
> [Where do you get hold of them?] From burglaries, man. You go into a home and find the guns. All the time. Guns. They're right there.

There are very serious crime problems in this country and you must take steps to prevent yourself and your loved ones from becoming victims. Guns, however, are so deadly that you or someone you love is apt to become a victim of your very own gun.

Few private citizens have the necessary continuous training and day-to-day experience to handle loaded guns. What is at question here is not only the ability to use a gun under normal conditions. Far more important is the ability to use a gun in an emergency. You need continuous training to make the split-second decisions under extreme pressure that go with using a gun. You don't want someone you love killed by your gun.

When was the last time you had professional instruction in the use of a gun?

DOGS

Far safer than guns for your protection are dogs, especially trained dogs. Edward M. Davis is Chief of Police of Los Angeles and a member of the executive committee of the International Association of Chiefs of Police. This is what Chief Davis says about the use of dogs for home security:

> The best protection is a dog, and the two best types are the Doberman and the German shepherd. They are intelligent, usually gentle with the family, and fiercely protective. But raise them to be a bit reserved with people outside your immediate family.

A properly trained dog, even a fierce breed like the German shepherd or Doberman, will be a good family dog. A guard dog will cost about the same as an inexpensive alarm system (call it about $600) plus over $100 a year for food, shots, licenses, etc. (Attack dogs cost a few thousand dollars and are used almost exclusively in stores and industrial plants to corner an intruder until help comes.)

All dogs have some abilities unmatched by most alarm units and systems. Dogs can hear potential intruders and can smell them. Even the small breeds can be more reliable than any electronic equipment and can produce a bark or growl that will both alert you and make any burglar turn his tail.

But there are dogs who "help the burglar." I used to think that was just a joke, dogs helping burglars. Then I spoke to a burglar. Roger, who claims "thousands" of hits, loved to meet a dog in a home he burglarized:

> I love dogs. They help me. I get into a home and they wag their tails and lick me. Never any trouble with dogs. Never. They help me. They warn me when someone's coming. They

can tell the sound of the motor, they can tell it's their master coming.

[Did you ever run into any German shepherds or Dobermans?] No. All kinds of dogs but not them.

German shepherds and Dobermans are the best, but if you're afraid of them, just about any dog can benefit from some training. When you are in the home and so is some stranger, you don't want your dog running and hiding under a living room table. You want help. If you love him just the cowardly way he is, consider buying a second dog. A watchdog.

A dog that will protect you is a dog that will bark and, if necessary, will bite. Of course you don't want him to harm innocent adults or children. While you can probably teach your dog to sit and "speak" and perform other tricks, a professional should handle potentially dangerous training.

But there are many shoddy trainers trumpeting their wares today. Always check with friends who have had their dogs trained, or contact the Better Business Bureau or lists of present customers of the dog schools you're considering.

You can take your dog with you when you walk, day or night, and when you drive a car. You'll be safer, even if you just have a small, untrained dog who will at least bark.

And when in the house or apartment, give your dog a full run of all the rooms. If he's locked in one area, he'll have a hard time protecting the home from intruders and will never be able to protect you from danger.

FAMILY MEMBERS AND BABY-SITTERS

All the caution you use with doors, windows, keys, lights, sounds, and callers can be defeated if others in your home are not just as careful. Whether they are adults or children, roommates or guests, you'll have to impress upon them the need to practice crime prevention or you won't be secure.

Baby-sitters can also be the weak link in your chain of home security. Many parents will discuss safety habits with their children and even their guests, but not the baby-sitter. "We'll just be going out for a few hours so there's no point to it." That's a too frequent attitude. Not only is the baby-sitter left in charge of the home, she often is the sole protection for the children. Take a few minutes to let your sitter know exactly how you want the home run. Let her know you're concerned about her and your children's well-being and she'll appreciate your instructions.

Tragically, there are times when a baby-sitter can be a threat to your family, for there are cases of child molesters who are baby-sitters. In all the instances I know of, the baby-sitters are teen-age boys. So hire only girls or women. (Chapter 13 has a fuller discussion of this subject.) Of course it's always safest also to know your sitter before you allow her into your home. Some people, however, rely on baby-sitting services and have good results.

PHONE CALLS

Detective Larry Carr of New York says, "It's your phone, so use it on your terms. If you don't know the caller, don't give out *any* information about yourself."

You won't want to tell a stranger your name, address, age, telephone number, if you are alone or when you will be out. All of that is common sense, yet offenders have a way of tricking some people:

> I had some baby furniture I wanted to sell so I put up a little notice on a bulletin board in a supermarket. I also told some friends and a few came over to look but we couldn't agree on a price.
>
> Then I got a call from a woman I didn't know who wanted to see the crib and stroller, the highchair. . . . She said she needed just about everything. She said she'd like to come over the following morning but I told her that wasn't convenient because I had a doctor's appointment and some errands to do in the morning.
>
> I returned home about lunchtime the following day and found that I'd been burglarized.

If a stranger is on the phone, don't say when you won't be home. Instead, be ambiguous. Say, "That's not a good time for me, how about . . . ?" Don't say why it isn't a good time. Similarly, if your man isn't home with you, don't tell that to someone you don't know calling for him. Simply say, "He's not available right now. Please let me have your number so he can call you back."

Everyone in your home—children, guests, and baby-sitters very much included—should follow these rules. Sometimes a person who dials your number "by mistake" will try to learn your number. Don't give it. Instead, ask what number he's calling, then tell him he'd better try again.

Women should have only their initials and last name in the phone book, not Miss, Mrs., or Ms. There are weirdos who go through the phone book looking for women to call, so don't let your listing assist them.

Crank calls or calls where no one replies when you answer the phone should be hung up on immediately. The crank calls may be from pranksters, but those where no one speaks from the other end may be from a burglar trying to find out if you're home, or from a "breather" who gets a charge out of hearing women's voices.

Persistent wrong numbers, crank or mysterious calls should be reported to the police and the phone company. You may want to change your number or have it unlisted.

The police and phone company usually have telephone stickers with emergency numbers to attach to your phone. Get these stickers and use them. Or, if 911 is in use in your area, make sure everyone knows that it brings help. Teach all your children to dial O in an emergency and that the operator will help them get the police or fire department.

Obscene calls are very disturbing but almost always committed by someone afraid of meeting women and very unlikely to physically harm anyone. Hang up on such a call immediately and notify the police. If you have a metal police whistle, keep it by the phone. Should another obscene call come, blow the whistle into the phone.

If everyone in your home is cautious about phone calls, careful with the doors and windows, keys, locks, and callers, you will all be safer. You won't have to worry about people like Owen:

At thirteen, Owen was large and strong for his age. That was when he started burglarizing homes. At fifteen, he realized that there were better things in homes than just TVs and stereos and jewelry. There were girls.

For the past year, he has been carefully selecting homes, entering, quietly getting a few objects together, then stealing into the bedroom of a teen-age girl. He would threaten her against calling out, then would rape her one, two, even three times.

The police don't know how many girls were his victims, six surely, but probably substantially more. Owen is now in a hospital for the criminally insane. Before he was admitted, he told police that every home he broke into either had one door unlocked or so poorly locked that he could force it open with his weight.

4

Apartment Buildings

"Apartment buildings are cities within a city. People come and go, move in and move out, and shut their doors. They don't know each other and, frankly, they don't care."

These are the words of an apartment-house dweller in the Midwest. There have been several petty thefts and two burglaries this year in his luxury apartment building. If his words are true of your apartment building, then you also have problems with theft and burglary or you may have them soon.

People aren't the only answer to crime, for both caring and uncaring people can be fooled. But the Chicago Police Department gives the following information: "Fifty per cent of crimes in high-rise buildings are due to failure to provide goods locks . . . and failure to use them!"

All the best hardware and electronic equipment won't do any good if people open the entry door for strangers, if they automatically press the door buzzer to let in unknown parties, if they don't have tough locks on their doors and don't use them. Why should you bother? Because people like Russ are at work every day.

Another of the cocky former burglars, Russ is a lanky young-looking man in his mid-twenties. His specialty was apartment buildings and he's happy to talk about them:

> They're door-to-door homes. That's the way I look at them, door-to-door homes. No trees or fences or dogs or cops patrolling. Homes on top of homes next to homes next to homes. That's why I used to work them.
>
> I'd walk into a building empty-handed, then, a few minutes later, I'd walk out with furs and cameras and radios and jewelry.
>
> [You'd just walk out with them?] In suitcases, man. I'd put all the stuff in suitcases.
>
> [How did you get into the building?] Through the front door. I'd wait around for someone to open it, then I'd go in.
>
> [While they were going in or coming out?] Uh-huh. One time I was a little high and I had this bag of groceries with me. I walked to the door and pretended to fumble with some keys. Some dude opened the door for me.
>
> [How did you choose which apartments to hit?] I'd watch the corridor. If there were people moving around, I'd try another. If not, I'd listen at doors to see if I could hear anyone.
>
> [What would happen if someone in another apartment saw you carrying things out?] Hell, I'd turn to the door and say, "See you, honey. I'll be back Friday," and walk off with the suitcases.

The impersonal nature of apartment buildings aids burglars as well as thieves, muggers, and rapists. Because people don't know who belongs in the building, they don't know who doesn't. And you can't tell by appearances, since a burglar like Russ or anyone else can dress nicely and fool you.

This chapter will discuss points not already covered on burglary as they relate to apartment buildings. If you live in such a high-rise building, please reread the preceding chapters, too, for they contain information that is relevant.

But unlike the earlier chapters, this discussion will also include thieves, muggers, and rapists who prey on the tenants and the property of tenants. While burglary is a hair-raising experience, mugging and rape are far more upsetting. Muggers use the display of weapons or threats of force or actual force to take money or other valuables from you. A substantial percentage of all muggings occurs indoors in hallways, elevators, basements, and inside houses and apartments.

There are cases in police records of burglars and rapists who live in apartment buildings and attack fellow tenants. Moreover, the tenants sometimes don't bring the problem to the attention of the police for months! The desire "not to get involved" often extends even to those victims who are already involved. The police cannot act until they know a problem exists. And since there are times where you and you alone must act for yourself, it is possible that you might be the one to notify the police of a problem.

OUTSIDE APARTMENT BUILDINGS

But for this discussion, we'll say that any and all threats to the security of an apartment building are posed from complete strangers. That's the situation in almost all cases.

The best protection for the entrance to an apartment building is provided by doormen. They get to know the occupants of the building and, unless they are kept too busy walking dogs and such, they carefully screen entrants. Private guards are a good second choice, for they, too, screen entrants. These guards, however, are often rotated from assignment to assignment so they may not get to know the building's occupants.

The expense of doormen or guards is, however, prohibitive to the tenants and the landlords of the great majority of apartment buildings. Closed-circuit television, with cameras covering entrances, hallways and garages, is also excellent, and also costly, for all but the very wealthy.

Most of us must rely on ourselves, the cooperation of fellow tenants, and a working relationship with the landlord and his agents.

Hopefully the front entrance faces a street where it can be observed by passers-by and by people across the street. If the main entrance is off an alley, you have less protection.

While the large apartment buildings in all major American cities usually have little or no shrubbery obscuring the entrance, some smaller apartment buildings do have plants and trees that can conceal a thief, mugger, or rapist. As with shrubbery near doors of a home, this should at least be trimmed if possible. Further action on the part of the landlord probably won't be taken unless and until there has been some trouble. And that's not crime prevention. If you are concerned by shrubbery near the entrances to your apartment building, make your views known.

Lights, as you know, are a major deterrent to crime. From dusk and on through the night, all entrances should be flooded with light to protect you when you enter and exit.

Parking areas for the building, either above ground or underground, should also be flooded with light. Even with good light, some police departments recommend that a male friend meet a woman who drives home at night and parks near or under an apartment building.

The doors to the outside must always be kept locked. Sometimes, however, the doors to underground garages or to service areas are left open for periods of time. This invitation to an intruder will, sooner or later, bring anyone from mischievous kids to a rapist into your building.

The doors(s) to the roof should also be kept locked at all times. From the outside, it should need a key to be opened so that intrusion is deterred. This is especially true if the roof of your building is so close to other buildings that a man can walk or jump across. Slide bolts on the inside or doors to the roof are an alternate if fire laws do not permit a conventional lock. But slide bolts must be bolted shut each time they are used. Sometimes people are careless.

This is where you and other security-minded tenants come in. Any lock on every outside (or inside) door can be abused if people don't care. The door itself must be strong and its lock must be able to withstand attempts at loiding. Unfortunately, many door locks are spring latch, not dead bolt. And spring-latch locks can usually be loided. Make it known that a dead-bolt lock should be installed instead. If the landlord won't provide the money for it and the tenants don't see the need, perhaps an inexpensive jimmy guard or face plate can bolster the security of the spring-latch lock.

If the door at the front entrance is operable solely by a bell-and-buzzer system, the apartment building is vulnerable. Most newer buildings have voice communication between the front door and the apartment so that the occupant can identify the caller. Although safer, this identification system is misused by many tenants. If you know of people in your building who automatically open the front door when the bell rings in their apartment, talk to them. The M.O. (modus operandi) of some burglars is to yell "postman" into the intercom systems of various apartments until one opens the door. Then the burglars can plunder any unit.

Russ and other criminals simply wait for someone entering or exiting the building to open the door for them. If you notice tenants doing that, talk with them. Detective Larry Carr of the Crime Prevention Section of the New York Police Department maintains that in far too many instances people just open doors and let strangers in. "Always question anyone who wants to enter with you. You might say, 'May I help you find someone?' It might turn out that the person you've questioned is actually a tenant. Fine. They'll appreciate the fact that you're trying to protect them, too. And tell them that."

If you need a little help, have a sign installed over or near the door saying "Key or buzzer must be used" and simply point to the sign as you close the door leaving the stranger outside. This may be hard for children, however, who have been taught to be polite. Explain to them why this is necessary. If you are able to develop what the New York police call "a challenging spirit," you'll find that it will spread to others. And it will keep some illegal intruders outside. Simply ask, "May I help you find someone?"

In many buildings, the door to the street is unlocked and leads to an outer lobby. Separating the outer lobby from the interior of the building is the locked door and in this outer lobby are the unprotected mailboxes. Mail thieves can attack these mailboxes when social security, welfare, or other checks arrive. If this is a problem, have the mailboxes moved within the secure portion of the building and give the mailman the key to a "key keeper." Key keepers are steel boxes that are mounted near or on the locked door; they contain the door key. One special key opens the key keeper of your building plus the other buildings along the mailman's route so he can easily deliver the mail.

While infrequent mail thefts may not motivate your landlord to move the mailboxes inside, perhaps the threat of muggings will. Many muggers wait for women to come down for the mail and then grab the checks from them. Often the woman gets hurt because she doesn't want to give up her check.

Both the mailboxes and, on occasion, building directories are often located in the outer lobby. In warm parts of the country, many smaller apartment buildings have no lobbies at all. The mailboxes and any directories face the street or a driveway. If there's no way to change their location, make sure their information doesn't communicate the fact that you're a woman. Use only your initials and last name on your mailbox and the directory. If your last name is not common in the immediate area, use it only.

Tenants of the first and second floors and the top floor must take more crime-prevention measures than those in the middle. The crime-prevention sections of several police departments advise this because illegal entry is possible from the ground or the roof into the apartments of these bottom and top floors. All windows on these floors (except those facing the fire escape) should be secured with window locks (keyed or keyless) that are strong. As with house windows, however, it is best to have keyless window locks on bedroom windows of ground-floor apartments to allow for escape if there's a fire.

There are some definite precautions to take if you live in a building with an exterior fire escape. Seldom will a burglar climb up or down several stories of a fire escape: it's too noisy. But it is always best to have a keyless window lock on any windows on or even near the fire escape. You want the lock keyless so you or a child can open it quickly in an emergency, but you also want it strong so that it keeps strangers out. Even if a window is not on the fire escape but near it, have that window secured. Why? Because the New York Police Department has cases on file of burglars who leaned six feet from the fire escape to an open window and climbed in!

Metal gates that slide open and closed for use in windows near fire escapes are seldom approved by fire departments. Although they are in use, for example in New York City, one detective has told me, "There is no such thing as an approved metal gate for a window in a private residence. It is against the law." Use a keyless window lock instead.

INSIDE APARTMENT BUILDINGS

Although we are now talking about the interior of an apartment building, there are many parallels with a neighborhood. Some neighborhoods are clean, well-lit, safe areas, containing the homes of proud, careful people. Others are the opposite. They are dirty, poorly lit, crime-ridden communities where people have lost their pride and cower in fear of the night and the day.

Apartment buildings with refuse in the corridors, graffiti on the walls, dark corners or poorly lit hallways are also apartment buildings that attract crime. If your apartment building is not like this, even if it is more like a comfortable neighborhood, there are ways to make it safer.

Your building must have strong illumination throughout its interior. This includes the entrance and lobby as well as all corridors. Burned-out lights or sockets with no lights should be reported immediately. If the illumination from the lights is not strong enough, make it known that you want light bulbs with a higher wattage. If the landlord won't give them to you, get together with some tenants and chip in for better bulbs. In the unlikely event that the landlord finds out about the switch (probably because of a slightly higher electric bill), a call or just the threat of a call to building inspectors might make him leave the new bulbs alone.

In addition to being well lit and clean, lobbies with plate-glass windows should not have drapes. There should, instead, be an unobstructed view to the outside. The reason for this is explained by Detective Carr: "Drapes in lobbies of apartment houses can hide people who are inside and waiting for women. Get rid of the drapes."

In apartment buildings with elevators, the interior stairways are seldom used. This, combined with the fact that many double as interior fire escapes and are soundproof, means that women should avoid using them. Of course these stairways should be well lit and free from debris, but because of the chance of some stranger loitering in them, women should use the elevators.

If building codes allow, and they usually do, one-way doors should be used on the interior stairways (assuming that there is an elevator). These doors would open outward on the ground floor and the roof only, and open inward on the floors in between. This arrangement would mean that people on the ground floor would have to use the elevator (particularly good if the elevator is manned) while someone who enters the stairway from a middle floor must exit either at the roof or the ground floor. A stranger, therefore, cannot use the stairway to burglarize apartments on various floors.

But he can use an unmanned elevator, and most apartment houses have elevators that are unmanned. Other strangers, be they rapists, child molesters, muggers, or responsible guests of tenants, also use the elevators. Elevators are a means of transportation, similar to buses and subways. But the best way to think about an elevator is as a car and you as a hitchhiker.

I assume you don't hitchhike and wouldn't, except in an extreme emergency. (If I'm wrong, please read Chapter 11, where I have some ideas that may make hitchhiking a little bit safer.) While you might enter an elevator with men who make you feel uneasy, you'd never enter a car with them. So, if the situation arises where you are uncomfortable at the thought of the door closing on you with a particular man or men inside, just step out. Or don't get in in the first place.

The same is true if you are riding in the elevator and someone you'd rather not ride with gets in at an intermediate floor. Simply walk out.

A great many women today are strong enough to do this. They don't need an excuse to mumble, nor do they need to fear hurting a strange man's feelings. There could be a million reasons why you want to get off and a stranger doesn't need to know one of them. Your safety is the only thing that counts. Even if there is not the least sign of an overt threat to you, don't get in the elevator or do walk out.

Some women or young girls, however, will need an excuse. They want some face-saving device to excuse what might be considered "odd" behavior. If that's the way you are, okay. Just make sure you're safe. You can say, "Oh, I almost forgot" and get out, or you can say, "I'll visit her now" and get out, or you can simply say, "Excuse me" and get out. You can use these same phrases to avoid getting in. Think and say and do whatever makes you most comfortable. If you know you're going to be tense for the duration of the ride, then avoid the ride. It's not worth it. And it's certainly not worth any chance, even the slightest, of being mugged or molested or raped.

The following case history was told to me by a detective:

> The young woman kissed her husband good-by and left their fifteenth-floor apartment. She got into the vacant elevator and pushed the button for the first floor. On the fifth floor, a young man got in. Something about him made her wary.
>
> It wasn't his appearance, for his clothes were okay and he was clean shaven. She didn't know what it was but she was "a little on edge." He pressed the second-floor button and she relaxed a little, thinking he must be a tenant visiting someone or going back to his own apartment.
>
> But when the elevator stopped at the second floor, he looked out, saw that no one was there, and pulled a knife on the young woman. He forced her out of the elevator, forbade her to scream, and took her to the stairs. There he sexually molested her.

This woman may have felt "a little silly" had she left the elevator at the fifth floor when the man got on. After all, she may not have known anyone on the fifth floor and would have had to stand there all alone.

Yes, but only for a minute or two. The detective told me that now her husband rides down with her. That's an excellent idea for you. Whenever possible, have a man you trust ride the elevator with you. If you think that would be putting him out, then when someone enters an elevator and you're uncomfortable, put yourself out.

Most of the time, elevators go to basements. When you are on the ground floor and want to go up, make sure the elevator is going up and not about to go down to the basement before it goes up. "Every elevator has a cycle," explains Detective Larry Carr. "If you get in before it has completed its cycle, it will take you down to the basement where someone could be waiting."

The cycle can be changed so that, for example, after a certain hour the only access to the basement is by the stairs. There are a number of ways that this can be done, but they are all technical and within the jurisdiction of the landlord or his agents. "What you can do," continues Detective Carr, "is to get into the elevator, push the basement button, then get out until the elevator completes its cycle and returns to you."

Elevators should have mirrors if, before entering, you are not able to see the entire interior. Before you get in, you want to see who the other "riders" are and decide whether or not you want to ride with them. It's your choice. Though it may not help much, you are always a little safer if you stand next to the control panel. If attacked, you can push the emergency or several floor buttons.

A detective with the New York Police Department's Assault and Homicide Section has this final work on elevators: "After you've gotten down the elevator safely, give two buzzes to your husband before you walk out the front door of the building."

If no other women are in the basement or the laundry room, consider it dangerous. Especially at night, but any time of the day, too. Many of the forcible rapes inside apartment buildings take place in basements or in laundry rooms. When you go to either of these areas, have a friend with you. A man or another woman will make the time spent there more enjoyable and it will help to prevent a possible crime.

Before you get off the elevator to walk down a corridor, you want that corridor well lit and you want it free of loiterers. The corridor is like a street: look both ways before you cross. Perhaps you won't cross, you'll walk down it instead. But look both ways first. And if there are corners into which you cannot see, make it known that you want mirrors installed. You don't want to get off an elevator before you can see every place in the corridor where someone could be lurking.

If someone is in the corridor and you get "bad vibrations" from him, don't get out. Stay in the elevator. Or, if a trusted friend lives near the elevator and you're sure he or she is home, go to their door. One expert, with fifteen years in Homicide and Assault, has seen "far too many cases of a man in the hallway, the woman leaves the elevator and rushes to her door but he gets to her first and takes her inside her own apartment."

When you have a hard day and can't wait to get home to your apartment and relax, more than mere suspicions are going to be necessary before you'll refrain from leaving the elevator and going to another floor. Or before you'll bother some friend who may have had just as hard a day.

A man walking in the corridor probably means no harm to you or anyone else. The situations we're talking about are rare. But when they do happen, they are often traumatic. If you take a few minutes to practice prevention, you will probably never be a victim.

When you move into a new apartment, ask yourself, "I wonder how many people have lived here before?" If the answer is one or one hundred, you should have the locks re-keyed. You have no idea how many of the former tenants have keys or have lost keys or who else might have keys. And don't forget, these are keys to *your* apartment. A licensed locksmith can re-key your locks for a nominal fee. Or, if the only lock on your doors is a spring latch, you should have a dead bolt installed. Your doors should also have an interviewer so you can see who's on the other side before opening up.

You might want to put a combination lock and alarm on your door (see Chapter 3 for more information on locks). Some apartment dwellers, however, think, "Why should I put anything on the door since I'm only renting?" Locks and their installation cost money, but the simple answer to that question is that you live inside. And you want to be as safe as possible.

You want to be sure to double lock your apartment when you step out, even if you're only going across the corridor to visit a neighbor for a second. Double locking your doors should become a habit. You should habitually double lock your doors when you are inside, too. Burglars most frequently jimmy or loid doors open, but this can't be done if you have a dead bolt or auxiliary lock. Other burglars simply walk down a long corridor checking each door to find one that's unlocked. Because that method works so often, it is the second most popular way for burglars to enter apartments.

You also want to be in control of all the keys to your apartment, but you're probably not. In fact, a great many people may be able to walk right in to your apartment any time of the day or night because they have duplicates of your keys. Re-keying your locks will eliminate duplicate keys in the hands of past tenants, but what about the landlord, the super, or other agents?

The building superintendent will want a key to your apartment. In some states, however, there is no law that says he must have a copy of your key. So check the laws of your state. If you must or want to give the super a key, one detective has this advice: "Put the key in an envelope, seal it, and sign your name over the seal. Make sure the super leaves you a note if he has gone into your apartment. Then you get the key back from him, put it in another envelope, seal and sign it."

Is there a need for this caution? You bet. While some supers keep apartment keys locked in a safe, many others just have them hanging in rows on the walls of their office. When a burglar breaks into this office, he takes all the keys and has the run of every apartment in the building.

One night when I was with Lieutenant Jim Motherway and his associates in the Citywide Anticrime Squad, he had a feeling that something was wrong in a parked car he had just passed. He circled around the block, came back behind the parked car, and got out. He and his men surprised two men in the parked car. These men carried guns and five hundred apartment keys. Two nights before, these two men had knocked off twenty-two apartments in just one building with the use of the keys. Unfortunately, this is not rare and that is why officials give you the advice about putting your key in an envelope, sealing it, and signing over the seal. The super must be made to account for your key.

If you don't want to give your key to the super and there's no state law that says you must, give it to a trusted neighbor and tell the super who has it. Or sign a paper allowing the super to break down your door in case of emergency. If he yells that he needs access to your apartment, the letter authorizing him to bust through your door should be enough. And it is very, very likely that he'll take you up on it. It is far more likely, on the other hand, that a key left with him will fall into another's hands.

Some supers will have a master key that lets them into every apartment. That's another reason you will want your own auxiliary lock on your door. When he asks for a duplicate key, stand up for your rights. After all, who lives in your apartment?

Any window on the fire escape should have a strong but keyless lock so that it can keep illegal intruders out but allow you or your children to exit rapidly in an emergency. Any window with access, no matter how difficult, from a tree, from the roof, or from a ladder should have a strong keyed window lock or window stops that allow it to open only a few inches.

As soon as you move into an apartment, get to know your neighbors. If you don't particularly like them, okay, but you can help each other. Get to know who lives where, plus their names and telephone numbers. Know them well enough so that you can go to them in an emergency.

Try to develop at least a nodding acquaintance with the other people on your floor. Before you walk down the corridor, you want to know who lives on this floor and who is a stranger.

If there is a tenant association in your apartment building, join it. Persuasion is about the only way to get all the people in the building to practice crime prevention, and tenant associations are an excellant means to that end. While some facets of protection are up to you (avoiding elevator rides when suspicious, going to the laundry room with a friend), others need the muscle of many people to have power against the landlord. Better interior and exterior lighting, stronger locks on exterior doors, peepholes in all apartment doors (it's the law in New York City), these and other costly measures have a better chance of being supplied when there's a tenant association.

Tenant patrols are another idea that helps deter crime in apartment buildings. Usually two men work together, either checking parking lots, stairways, laundry, basement, storage, and other rooms, or sitting in the lobby at a desk taking the names and destinations of visitors to the building. Since the tenant patrols do a very good job, get your man to join one. If necessary, you start one.

The point is, where tenants are concerned, crime is deterred. Tenant associations and patrols, questioning of visitors to the building, good lights inside and out, all of these crime-prevention measures are observable by burglars, muggers, and others. Then word gets around that your building is pretty tight and criminals stay away.

But when it comes to your safety and that of your loved ones, don't pass the buck. Don't let a tenant association take care of your welfare. And don't let the lack of a tenant association keep you from acting. If others in the building won't cooperate with you, or the landlord or super is giving you a hard time, call in the police. Many police departments have special units of officers specially trained in crime-prevention measures for apartment buildings. Find out about these experts in your area.

Since most burglars come right through the front door, you arrange for a sign near that door saying "Key or buzzer must be used" and do your damnedest to get other tenants to stick to it.

Because you want your neighbors to help you when there's trouble, help them. Says a New York detective, "If there seems to be something unusual going on in your neighbor's apartment, call the police. You don't have to investigate, the police will. And if it turns out to be an unnecessary call, the police aren't going to scold you, and they're not going to charge you."

Look out for your neighbors as you look out for yourself and your loved ones. Your apartment building is a neighborhood. The more cooperation there is among the tenants, the safer you and your loved ones are.

You'll probably find some people who don't want to cooperate. They haven't the time, they don't think there's a problem, they're just not interested, whatever. Give them this chapter to read. If the person in question is a man, make sure he also reads the following story.

I talked with a man about a week after a crime occurred in his apartment building. Incidentally, his building has only two floors and a total of sixteen apartments, but he doesn't know a quarter of the tenants:

> I was watching a football game and there was a knock on the door. Seems this guy wants me to help move a TV out to his van. He said he was a repairman moving my neighbor's set out to be repaired only it weighed too much for one man to move.
>
> It was the fourth quarter and I didn't want to go out so I offered him a beer and told him I'd help him when the game was over. He was impatient, sort of nervous. He said he was way behind in his service calls.
>
> Anyway, I went with him to the apartment. I figured the neighbor would help us too, you know, but he wasn't there. And me, my mind was too much on the game to wonder how the repairman got into the apartment if the owner wasn't there.
>
> So, to make a long story short, I helped this burglar move the TV out of the apartment, down the stairs, and into his van!

Right now, make a note of where you can get help quickly if you need it. Which neighbors can you contact, how fast can you get to the superintendent, where are the fire alarms in the building? Have this information before you need it and you may be able to allay some fears, prevent a crime, or help catch a thief.

5

Confrontation with a Burglar

It was 10:30 at night. It was a Wednesday, a little over a month ago. Jack [her husband] was out of town and I was reading a book in bed. My two girls were asleep, everything was quiet until I heard a noise.

It sounded like the side door opening, the one Jack uses at night. I thought he was surprising me coming home a day early. I grabbed a robe and walked quickly to the hall.

There was a man, not Jack, a stranger. He saw me and pulled out a gun.

I screamed. It was a reflex reaction, I didn't think about it. He told me to shut up and I shut up. He asked if there were kids in the house and I told him there weren't. He saw one of Casey's dolls and told me to get the kids.

I tried to be calm. I woke my children up and tried to explain things. I guess I took too long because the man came into the bedroom and told us all to get into the bathroom.

I was sure he was going to kill us all. I think I was calm, after that first scream. I know neither of the girls cried and they would have if my fears really showed.

The man told us to remain quiet and stay in the bathroom. We did. A little later, I'd say after about five minutes, we heard the side door close. We waited a little and walked out of the bathroom. The house was a mess, lots of jewelry, some money, a few other things were gone. But we were unharmed.

"Residential burglars never really want to confront anybody," says an expert with the New York Police Department's Burglary and Larceny Section. Cases like the above are far from the majority but this and many, many others are on file with various police departments.

Burglars make mistakes. The man in the above case history didn't see that the bedroom light was on. That light shone out the back of the house. He looked only at the front and side and decided that it was empty. There are also cat burglars who work at night whether or not the house is vacant, and hot burglars who will go into bedrooms where people are sleeping to get money and jewelry that otherwise wouldn't be there. As you've seen on television, there are also burglars who go to a home when there's a party and steal the coats that are left in bedrooms.

Since it's so much easier for a burglar simply to find a vacant home that is not properly protected, experts estimate that only about 3 per cent will enter a home when people might be there. And most of these burglars will do everything they can to avoid being seen or confronted by you.

So relax as you read this. There's very little chance that you'll actually need this information, but should such a situation arise, you'll know what to do.

Up until this point in the book, we've been talking about prevention. You now know the very best ways to prevent a burglar from entering your house or apartment when you're away. More importantly, you know how to deter illegal entry when you or your loved ones are at home. Now we talk about confrontation.

I asked several burglars two questions about a confrontation with a man or woman. First, what should the man or woman be sure *not* to do. Secondly, what should the man or woman be *certain* to do.

Every burglar answered that the man or woman should "be sure to stay out of the way." *Never* get between a burglar and his exit and *never* try to stop him from leaving.

Roger elaborates:

> Before a burglar enters a place, I'm talking about the smart ones now, he knows how he's going to get out. More than getting money or stuff, he wants to get out okay. So he knows before he goes in.
>
> [What about guys who aren't so smart?] The amateurs, the kids, they act on impulse. Maybe they think about getting out, maybe they just think about scoring.

If a burglar hasn't thought about his exit and sees someone in the house or apartment, he'll start thinking fast. Then he'll bolt for the nearest door, so get out of his way.

In answer to the second question, what should a man or woman be sure to do, all the burglars answered the same way: "Call the cops!"

Larry elaborates:

> Most of the time I carried a gun in my pocket. I never had to use it. I never even took it out. I don't think I would have used it. I don't think I would have shot anyone.

Don't bet your life on it! When Larry was in a home, his "heart was beating a thousand times a minute." He was scared. He was also in need of money for his narcotics habit. If someone had tried to prevent his escape, he would have used any means to get out, including his gun.

But you don't just avoid a confrontation, you *plan* to avoid it. You become psychologically prepared to act in such a way so that you protect yourself and your children and other loved ones from harm.

"How?" I asked an expert, Policewoman Cindy Miller of the Los Angeles Police Department. Policewoman Miller works undercover in vice operations. She works the streets and she also works houses, apartments, stores, and cars. She knows how to get out of just about any tight situation. "We vice operators who work undercover prepare ourselves for any situation by thinking, 'What if . . . ?' and trying to come up with answers."

This short, lively, pretty woman talks things over with her male and female associates and comes up with various plans. "First of all, we want to avoid trouble. That's where the 'What if . . . ?'s come in. I think it's a good technique for all women to use."

The reason Policewoman Miller has never been hurt is due in great part to forethought and precautions taken before she ever leaves police headquarters.

Take her advice. Ask yourself, "What if I came up the walk and found scratches on the front door near the lock?" "What if I opened the door to my apartment and found that I couldn't get in because, somehow, the door chain was engaged?" "What if we came home from vacation and found that one of the house windows was broken?" "What if I came home one night and had a feeling that something was wrong in my apartment?"

The answer in all of these cases is to get away from your house or apartment, go to any nearby phone, and call the police. Even if you only have a suspicious feeling that something is wrong, don't investigate. Leave that to the police.

"What if I get inside my home and then see that someone has ransacked the place?" "What if I get inside my home and see some stranger?"

The answer in both cases is, "Get out!" If the burglars have left, you don't want to enter and move, tidy up, or even touch anything as this might obscure fingerprints and other clues. And the burglar might still be inside in another room. If the burglars are there and you see them, leave.

The following case history comes from Massachusetts, but it could just as well be from your state:

> Mary Ann Hopkins, a twenty-six-year-old secretary, returned to her third-floor apartment and interrupted two teenage youths stealing her television. She challenged them.
>
> One of the intruders grabbed her from behind while the other struck her on the head with an iron crowbar. Neighbors heard her screams and one of the boys shouting, "Hit her again."
>
> Police found Miss Hopkins unconscious on the floor. She suffered a concussion and fractures of the wrist and hands. The youths fled with the TV and a radio.

"What if I'm upstairs or in another part of the house and I hear what might be a burglar?" "What if I'm walking through the house and I see a stranger in a room but he doesn't see me?"

To avoid confrontation, don't approach him, don't yell at him. Get out of the house quietly, if you can. But if children are inside with you and you can't get them out or there is not an exit for you, go to a phone. Call the police and stay on that phone until they arrive.

If you can't get to a phone, signal a neighbor. That may be as easy as knocking on your wall or ceiling. A better idea is to take some solid object (perhaps one of your shoes) and throw it through a window. The noise will attract attention and might scare the burglar away.

"What if I have a gun or a strong dog?"

"A burglary is not a life-and-death situation. Therefore, I do not advise the private citizen to turn a gun on a burglar." Those are the words of Sergeant Lee Kirkwood.

Why does he say that? "The burglar wants to get out when he sees people. So stand out of his way. If you have a gun, he might take it away and use it on you." Since the burglar is already on the wrong side of the law, he is prepared and willing to take chances you won't take. Avoid him.

And keep your dog away from him too. If the intruder turns and starts for you, then you want your strong dog for protection. You don't want your dog to attack him and get maimed or killed, leaving you defenseless. Keep the dog by your side.

"What if I'm asleep and I wake up to see a burglar in my room?"

A New York Police Department expert answers, "Pretend you're still asleep. It's very hard but that's the best thing. As long as he doesn't come near you or touch you, fake sleeping. Try to obtain a description of him. The minute he's gone, call the police and give them the description."

"What if I'm inside and someone is prowling around outside?"

Turn on some lights in different rooms. Make him think several people are home. If he's outside during the day, let him think a man is home even if you're alone. Let him hear you yell to your husband, "Dear, there's someone outside." If the man's presence makes you uncomfortable, call the police and describe the prowler to them. And just before you call them, again say to someone supposedly in the home with you, "I'm going to call the police."

"What if he's inside and I'm inside and he's closer to the exit than I am?"

Put other doors between you and him. Retreat into the home.

"What if he's inside and I'm inside with the kids and he has a gun?"

One New York detective says to keep this uppermost in your mind: "You can always replace property, you can never replace a life." The burglar is after property, he is not out to harm you or your children. If he is armed, do what he says. Make sure the kids follow your instructions. The best way to avoid any possible harm is to remain calm. Or, said the other way around, if you panic, harm may come to you or your loved ones. Don't scream or yell. Be calm. He'll either leave right away or, as in the case history that started this chapter, he'll tell everyone to get in one room, then he'll take some property and leave.

A question you probably won't ask but should, "What if I'm coming home and I'm not the least suspicious of a burglar inside?"

Ring your own doorbell. You don't want to surprise a burglar and you probably never will. But it takes only a second to ring your bell before you open the door. That second of prevention is worth it, isn't it?

6

After a Burglary

The burglar has fled, the confrontation is over. The next few moments are vital.

If you can go to a window to see how he flees (by foot, by car, with others) plus the direction he takes, you have invaluable information to give the police. Call them. Use the emergency number, tell them you have a burglary to report, and try to remain calm so you can speak slowly and clearly.

The Metropolitan Police Department of Washington, D.C., asks that you give the following information:

Address of the incident
Description of the incident
Description of the subject and route of escape taken by the suspect
Car description and tag number where applicable
Any other details which may be of help to the police

After your call to the police, there will be a few moments of quiet before they arrive. You have two jobs to do. First, protect the scene of the crime. Don't let anyone touch anything or walk into the area where the burglar was. Secondly, take some paper and write down a thorough description of the man. The Des Moines Police Department offers the illustrations on pages 85–87 to help you describe the offender.

If he uses a car, supply any of the following information you can. Unless you're great at reading numbers fast, don't try to record them all. Get the first three and notice if it's out of state. Record as much as possible of the following:

COLOR   _____

YEAR   _____

MAKE   _____

BODY   _____

ANTENNA   _____

LICENSE   _____

And one last thing to write down before the police come are any objects the burglar touched.

When the police arrive, cooperate to the best of your ability. Give the notes you've made to the police. Answer their questions. They will request a list of articles that are missing. You can prepare such a list more quickly *and* have a chance of getting the goods back to you if you have already itemized the valuables in your home and engraved identifying numbers on them.

In Chapter 2, Operation Identification and Computer Identification System were mentioned. When you place decals on the doors of your home that say your possessions have been marked for police identification, you tell potential burglars that your goods will be hard to fence. Because your items are marked, time is needed to rub out the markings. The burglar has no time, the fence doesn't want to bother, and the scratched-out area will raise the suspicions of any buyer. Before he gets to the fence, the burglar has another problem with properly marked goods. If he's stopped by the police, they have proof that this merchandise is stolen.

The main benefit in marking your possessions is deterrence. Among the many cities to adopt Operation Identification is New Orleans. Burglaries in the first three months of 1971 were 39 per cent higher than the first three months of 1969. So in April of 1971, Operation

TELL IT LIKE IT WAS...
DESCRIBE ONLY WHAT YOU SAW!

HOW TO DESCRIBE A PERSON

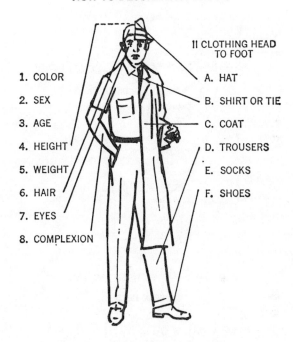

II CLOTHING HEAD
TO FOOT

1. COLOR
2. SEX
3. AGE
4. HEIGHT
5. WEIGHT
6. HAIR
7. EYES
8. COMPLEXION

A. HAT
B. SHIRT OR TIE
C. COAT
D. TROUSERS
E. SOCKS
F. SHOES

ADDITIONAL TIPS TO HELP MAKE
REMEMBERING MORE ACCURATE

- Look for easily spotted, distinguishing marks or physical characteristics, such as tattoo, scar, glasses, limp, loss or impairment of a limb, facial twitches, etc.

- Listen for a specific speech and/or vocal characteristics, such as an accent, repeated use of certain words or phrases, extremely poor (or correct) grammar, etc.

- Notice hands. Are any fingers missing? Did the criminal wear any rings, bracelets or a watch?

- Try to determine general build, height, weight and approximate age by comparing the suspect to someone who is known to you.

HOW TO DESCRIBE THE FACE

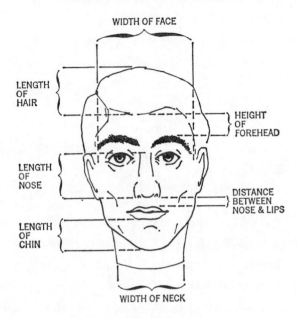

WIDTH OF FACE

LENGTH
OF
HAIR

HEIGHT
OF
FOREHEAD

LENGTH
OF
NOSE

DISTANCE
BETWEEN
NOSE & LIPS

LENGTH
OF
CHIN

WIDTH OF NECK

GENERAL SHAPE OF HEAD AND FACE

SHAPE OF HEAD

ROUND	TRIANGULAR	SQUARE

WIDTH OF HEAD

NARROW	NORMAL	WIDE

PLACEMENT OF THE EYES

WIDE APART	MEDIUM	CLOSE TOGETHER

DISTINCTIVE FACIAL FEATURES

EYES		
EYEBROWS		
NOSE		
MOUTH		
CHIN		
EARS		

HAIR STYLES

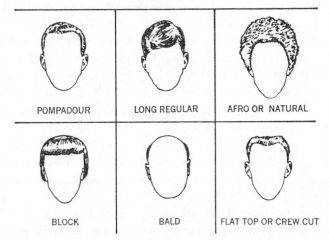

| POMPADOUR | LONG REGULAR | AFRO OR NATURAL |
| BLOCK | BALD | FLAT TOP OR CREW CUT |

Identification was started. At the end of 1971, the burglary rate in New Orleans for the entire year had dropped 3 per cent below that of 1969. Similar results have been achieved in other cities.

In some areas of the country, Operation Identification is called the Computer Identification System. The two methods are essentially the same, though in the Computer Identification System you always file a registration card with the local police. Dallas, for example, uses the Computer Identification System.

Your local police department will tell you what system they are using. (If they're using no such system, find out why.) Be sure to determine if you are to engrave your driver's license number (California, Texas, and Michigan) or your social security number (New York and Colorado). While police can retrieve information on your driver's license number any time of the day or night from a central state office, no such system is available for social security numbers out of Washington. So if you are to engrave your social security number, make sure you file it with your local police department.

It is possible to record only the serial number the manufacturer has placed on many (but not all) of your goods. But that only allows you to identify your goods when and if you ever see them again. Only 4 per cent of stolen goods is returned to its owners.

So use the Operation Identification or Computer Identification System decals outside all your doors and mark your social security or driver's license number on appliances, televisions, stereos, tools, cameras, and other valuables.

You can buy a small engraving tool for between $10 and $20. Some police departments lend them free for two or three days as do some organizations such as the National Exchange Club and the National Association of Insurance Agents. Etch your identifying number into a nonremovable part of the item near the manufacturer's serial number if possible.

It does take some time to mark each item, but it may very well prevent a burglary or, if you've already been hit, it may prevent a recurrence. Periodically, after you've brought other goods into your home, you'll want to etch them, too.

For furs, use indelible ink to mark your number on the inside of the skins where it will do no damage and also not readily be seen.

Some items can't be engraved. Money (keep it in the bank), jewelry (photograph less expensive jewelry, have costly items X-rayed), and many antiques are not covered by this system.

You may want to use the following form for your inventory record. If so, rip it out of the book or duplicate it so you can put this inventory list in a safe place. The Dallas Police Department has supplied this form for your convenience.

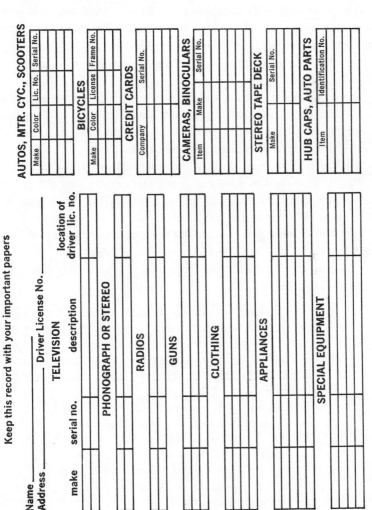

If you want more information about Operation Identification, you can contact its originator, Police Chief Everett Holladay (Ret.), Operation Identification Incorporated, P. O. Box 676, Monterey Park, California 91754.

With your inventory list in hand, you can quickly determine which items have been stolen and you can immediately give the police all the pertinent data on your valuables. The police will be glad to have your information and will have a much better chance of getting your goods back to you. Up until that time, the police will ask that you continue your cooperation by supplying any additional information and by identifying the suspects if and when apprehended.

The entire period after a burglary, from the first minutes to the last weeks or months, will be greatly simplified by the time you spend marking your goods. And, not incidentally, your records will also be very helpful when filing insurance claims.

When there has been no confrontation with a burglar but your home has been broken into and goods are missing, call the police and protect the scene of the crime until they arrive. Then give the police your information and cooperation.

That's straightforward enough, but what about an attempted burglary that doesn't succeed? Should the police be called?

The following case history was told to me by a stunning journalist in her mid-twenties:

> I drove in behind my building at about eight o'clock at night and went to my apartment. It has a private entrance on the ground floor. I opened the door, turned on the light, and thought I heard something. I didn't pay any attention, though, as I started walking through the living room. But then I became puzzled because I didn't see my TV.
>
> It's portable so my first thought was maybe I left it in the bedroom. I went to look and found no TV and no stereo, either. But I did find a bedroom window wide open and a screen ripped. I walked over to the window and there, in a little alley outside, were my TV, stereo, and a number of other things.
>
> Then it flashed through my mind: I'd come home just as my apartment was being burglarized!
>
> I turned and ran out of the bedroom, through the living

room, and out the door. I was going to get those burglars! Fortunately for me, I stumbled on the driveway. As I was getting up, I heard a car roar away from the curb. I hobbled over to the street but could distinguish nothing because the driver left his lights off.

I yelled to a friend in a nearby apartment. The two of us examined my stereo, TV, vacuum cleaner, camera, and a six-pack of beer that remained undamaged in the alley. We took everything back inside and drank the beer.

After about an hour and all those beers, my thoughts mellowed and I decided to call the police.

Even though nothing was actually taken, the police were grateful that the woman called. "Illegal entry is a crime and should be reported," says Detective Larry Carr. "Any crime and any attempt at crime, successful or not, should be reported."

Why bother the police when there has been no loss? Because a crime was committed (illegal entry) and another was attempted (burglary). Because a police investigation of the scene may yield information about the perpetrators, information that may help establish a pattern that can lead to their capture. Because the investigation may include neighbors who have seen or heard valuable information. Because the police will patrol your area frequently. And because "bringing it out in the open" will alert your neighbors and the entire neighborhood to the fact that a burglar is working in the area.

If those are not enough reasons, here's another: if you don't report it, word will get around that your home and your neighborhood are easy marks. Several burglary investigators have told me this and so have several former burglars. Larry, the hype who often carried a gun, met people on three different occasions who were intimately occupied:

> I'd test the house [ring the doorbell] then cut a back screen and start in with my partners right behind. Three times I got inside and there was a couple balling. They'd look up. I'd say something like, "Sorry, I guess this is the wrong house." I'd leave and they'd never report me.
>
> [How do you know they'd never report you?] Because a

day or two later I'd hit the house next door. They'd leave a
door or window wide open.

Reporting illegal entry or attempted burglary, or a burglary where
only a few minor items are taken, can offer the police valuable leads.
In the case of the young career woman, the responding officers were
displeased that she'd waited so long to call and that she'd touched
all the possessions that were in the alley. They also wanted to know
what she would have done had she actually confronted the bur-
glar(s). She didn't know. Neither did the officers. Both she and the
officers were glad there was no confrontation.

While calmly reading a book, it may be a little difficult to understand how a woman could think of running after one or more burglars in hopes of "getting" them. The undisciplined emotions of the
moment almost got *her* into serious trouble. It is, however, far harder
to understand the following case history. I'm told by police officers
that similar events occur daily. The speaker is an elderly woman:

> I forget what I was doing before I walked into my bedroom,
> but there was this young man holding some of my old jewelry.
> He was really a little boy and I was very surprised to see him.
> He was very cute.
> I asked him, "What on earth are you doing?" but he said
> nothing. He started to back away with the jewelry so I told
> him to put it down and get out of the house. He did.

This woman never reported this boy who, at the time, was eleven.
She didn't report him because, she later told police, "He was so cute."

That's only part of the story, though. This young burglar went on
to burglarize several homes in the area. When he was finally caught,
he had a little story to tell about the elderly woman. She said it
wasn't true, but the youth claimed he was such a smooth talker, that
after this old woman caught him, he turned things around and sold
her a stolen radio.

The elderly woman had a portable radio that the young burglar
claimed he'd sold her. There was no driver's license number or
social security number on it, and the woman claimed it as her own.
The boy may just have been boasting.

But every day, people all over the country buy stolen property.

And they do it knowingly. When the price is ridiculously low and a stranger is selling it in a parking lot or at your door, whatever story he's telling is almost surely a lie. This man or boy should be reported to the police immediately.

Yet, instead, many people would rather buy his merchandise. Sergeant Edward Powers of the New York Police Department has some choice words for people who buy stolen property: "If you buy a fifteen dollar TV, you're encouraging burglaries and you're contributing to the drug problem."

7

Vacations

Whether you're leaving for a few days, a few weeks, or several months, you make your vacation plans in advance. The minute you start planning your vacation, it's also best to start crime-prevention practicing.

Be careful about letting strangers know of your plans. When discussing your trip with friends, you won't want people nearby to overhear the conversation. You also won't want strangers to read about the times your home will be vacant so don't let newspapers publicize it.

Police departments all over the country, from New York to Miami to Los Angeles to Seattle, all have lists of things to do and not to do before you go away. One of the reasons for these helpful lists is a former burglar I'm calling Van. A gun freak and self-claimed rapist, he has served time for breaking into homes. His speciality has been vacant homes, homes where the owners were on vacation:

> You can tell. Newspapers lying around, milk cartons, flyers, no lights on. It's just like an invitation, which I gladly accept. [How can a person prevent such a burglary?] The whole

going-away bit. Cancel deliveries, have a neighbor pick up flyers, mow the lawn, shovel the drive, you know. Get some lights on. The whole bit. You just go right for a house that doesn't do these things. Every time. Why sweat about another house?

Van, who is short and thin and balding, is the cockiest ex-convict I talked with. He is also among the most candid and makes it imperative that you perform "the whole going-away bit." The Newton (Massachusetts) Police Department provides the basis of the following list:

Have the milkman and newspaper carrier stop making deliveries, but you needn't explain the cancellation.

Ask the mailman to hold your mail at the post office, deliver it to a neighbor, or forward it to you.

Leave a key with a friend. Ask him or her to check the inside of your home, also to change the positions of drapes, blinds, and shades.

Arrange with a neighbor to remove advertising and other flyers from your lawn, mailbox, or steps.

Leave some inexpensive toys or garden furniture around the house and ask a neighbor to change their positions periodically.

Tell the police when you are leaving and when you plan to return. A special watch will be made of your house during your absence.

Use automatic timers to turn lights and a radio on and off. Staggering lights (having them go on and off in different rooms at different times) is most effective.

Arrange to have a very conscientious neighbor boy mow the lawn or shovel the walk and driveway.

Tell the police which neighbor has a key and where you can be reached in an emergency.

Remove and store in a safe place all money, valuable jewelry, and other articles that can be easily stolen. Don't hide them within the home but remove them to a bank or storage vault or to the home of a good friend.

Inspect all doors and windows before leaving to make certain they are securely locked.

Look at your home objectively to see if it appears occupied or vacant.

Ask a neighbor to watch out for your home and report any suspicions to the police.

Much of the above is relevant to apartment tenants; the following should be added:

Tell your super when you are leaving and how long you will be gone.

Have a neighbor frequently jiggle your front door to see if it will open.

There are also a few things that you should *not* do:

Don't disconnect the phone. That's a tip-off that no one's there while an unanswered phone could mean that someone is inside but too busy to answer. Consider engaging a phone-answering service (human or machine) that provides no definite details about your absence. Or ask your telephone company if they will disconnect your phone *but* provide an automatic message that your phone is temporarily out of order.

Don't hide a key near a door for use in emergencies.

Don't close all curtains, shades, and blinds. Leave them in various positions from normal to almost closed so that an illegal intruder who is inside can be seen from the outside.

Don't shut the air conditioning or the heater off. Leave the air conditioning at about 75° and the heater at about 40°.

Don't set the trash cans out a few days early. This is a sure sign that you won't be home on trash-collection day. Have a neighbor or a boy set the trash out on the appropriate day.

This is a pretty long list of do's and don'ts, but Detective Larry Carr attests to its importance: "During the summer and during the winter, too, many people go off on vacation. If you don't take precautionary measures to protect your home, there's a good chance you'll find things missing when you return."

All of the do's and don'ts are aimed at creating one impression. Detective Carr continues, "The key is giving your home a lived-in appearance."

Any kid burglar can see that a home with mail and flyers piled up outside is vacant. Pros like Van also listen for air conditioners if it's hot or heaters if it's cold. If snow is on the window sills, a pro will deduce that no one is home, because there's no heat to melt this snow. For those with window air conditioners that don't work by thermostatic control, ask a neighbor to come in and turn them on when it's hot.

But isn't all of this a lot to ask of neighbors and other people?

"People are the most effective crime deterrent," says Sergeant Lee Kirkwood of the Los Angeles Police Department's Crime Prevention Section. "They know there's a need for action against crime, but most don't know what to do. The best thing is to help each other. You help them when they go on vacation, they help you when you go away."

That's the best answer for almost everybody. I know of a few people, however, who take a separate vacation from their spouses because they are so worried about burglary. A more positive and just as effective step is to have your vacation yet have your home occupied: have a house-sitter.

Among your friends, relatives, or associates are sure to be some single, young married, or middle-aged and trustworthy persons who would gladly have a little vacation of their own by living in your home while you're away. Of course you will want people who are not only honest but also careful with your possessions and con- scientious about following your home-security rules. House-sitters also enable you to keep your animals at home and not board them at a kennel and ensure that your plants will be cared for. If the dog must be walked or the plants given special care, the pool must be cleaned or other chores must be done, you'll probably want to pay the house- sitter some token fee. Otherwise, you can often find house-sitters for free.

If there's no one within the family or among close friends, try friends of relatives or friends of friends. You might also try a local hospital for the names of interns, the local police department for a young officer, a church or youth group or the housing office of a local college or university. If you do look for someone you don't know, take time to get to know them. You'll be leaving your home and all it means to you in their hands, so be sure you're comfortable with them.

Another idea is to swap homes with someone in another part of this country or in another country. You live in their home and they live in your home. Some travel agencies can give you more information, or contact one of the several organizations involved with house swapping, including Vacation Exchange Club, Inc., 663 Fifth Avenue, New York, New York 10022 or Adventurers for Living, P. O. Box 278, Winnetka, Illinois 60003.

Before you start out on your trip, you already know it's best to take as little cash as necessary. Instead, use credit cards and traveler's checks. But since both of these can be stolen, keep two separate records of the numbers of both credit cards and traveler's checks. Keep one record in a pocket that has neither the cards nor checks and another record with your luggage. You might want to take along a few personal checks, too. If you must carry large amounts of cash, consider using a money belt.

Wherever you go and whatever you do, don't display large amounts of cash or a great many credit cards. Do so and you're a walking advertisement for a mugger, pickpocket, or purse snatcher. (Chapters 8 and 9 discuss crime in the streets, in public transportation, and in cars.)

The locks on most luggage are made to keep honest people honest, not to keep dishonest people out. So don't buy expensive luggage thinking you'll have better protection for your valuables, because you probably won't. Have good luggage that will stand up to some rough handling, don't pack it too full or it might burst, and be there when your luggage is unloaded from a train or plane or bus. Have identification outside *and* inside your bags.

Airports and train and bus stations are prime areas for pickpockets and purse snatchers. A great many people from out of town carrying money and moving rapidly with many things on their minds provide the good pickings. When you enter one of these terminals, realize the potential danger and have your mind as free as possible of extraneous thoughts. Carry your pocketbook close to your body, preferably holding not its straps but its top or its body. If your man or son or brother carries his wallet in his back pocket, even if he buttons this back pocket, he is tempting pickpockets. The best place for a wallet is in an inside suit jacket pocket or a front pants pocket.

Now a bit of tricky advice. If you must carry large amounts of cash or small valuables and you won't use a money belt, be careful —don't call attention to yourself. Keep your purse held securely, or your wallet in your pocket, but don't keep checking it or touching it or tapping it. If you do, you will tell a purse snatcher you're nervous about something very valuable. In other words, use your knowledge about the dangers in transportation terminals to act for your own protection and build your own self-confidence.

If you travel by car, your luggage can attract thieves. (So can your car, but see Chapter 9 for that discussion.) The second major crime category in terms of frequency is larceny of $50 or above. Purse snatching, pocket picking, stealing auto accessories or articles from within cars, including luggage, all fit into this category. Over 1,800,000 cases were reported to the police last year.

While luggage in any car can attract thieves, luggage in a car with out-of-state license plates is especially enticing. Why? In addition to the valuables in all luggage, thieves know that out-of-staters will be reluctant to return to testify against them.

What to do? Keep your luggage in your motel room until just before you drive on. Don't pack up your car and leave it sitting while you go off to say good-by to friends or have a meal. If you have a trunk, use it. If you have a station wagon with little or no concealable space, consider an auto alarm. A blanket or other cover over valuables within your car may stop honest people from being tempted, but a young or professional thief will have a very good idea what's under the cover.

Hotel and motel rooms are best considered poorly protected. Your attitude should be that you are spending the night not in a private room but in a *public* room. Perhaps hundreds, even thousands of people have stayed in this same room, opened the same lock with the same key. Or did they keep their key and have you a duplicate? More disturbing is the fact that the management and help of hotels and motels usually use a master key: one key will let them into several rooms. If this key falls into the hands of a burglar, then your room is unsafe.

The best solutions are to carry as few valuables as possible, check what you can in the safe provided by the management, and take your own lock and key. Several companies make small locks that slide into doors and drawers. Some are keyless, others are keyed, and most can be purchased for between $3.00 and $6.00.

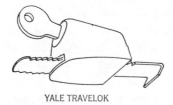

YALE TRAVELOK

When you enter your room, slip the lock into the door before you shower or relax or, of course, before you go to sleep. Otherwise, if you're taking a shower, it's possible for a burglar to loid the lock, slip in, and take some of your possessions in a very few minutes without you suspecting a thing.

But if you inset a keyed lock in your door, leave the key close-by in case you have to exit fast.

Before you leave the room, you can use the lock either on a closet to protect valuables hanging inside or on a top drawer. Use this lock only on a top dresser drawer. If used on a middle or bottom drawer, the one above can be removed and the "locked" drawer will be open.

Should you bother to buy and use a travel lock? Here's a case history from Florida. Although this burglar is not typical, hotel and motel burglaries are common today:

> She looks like a typical, nondescript grandma, with her gray hair and tennis shoes, but fifty-four-year-old Marsha Carter is anything but. She has been a burglar for several years.
>
> Posing as a maid, she has worked at several resort hotels and, when caught, had master keys for rooms in thirty-three hotels, most in Florida, but some from as far away as Kansas and Missouri. She also had credit cards, traveler's checks, forty pieces of quality jewelry, and two mink coats, one valued at $2,100.
>
> First unlocking a door and stealing into a room, this woman would then take the goods and run to the nearest post office.

After wrapping them carefully, she'd ship them off to a fence in the Midwest. She didn't run fast enough with the above valuables.

One of the reasons you may go on vacation is to see new sights and meet new people. Put in a negative fashion, that means to go to strange places and meet strangers. That isn't your attitude and I'm not suggesting it should be. But you may very well journey to unfamiliar cities where you know no one and where you should act cautiously.

A city street that has thousands of people and cars on it at five o'clock may be deserted at eight. A park that is beautiful and at peace during the day may be the scene of ugliness and violence at night. A section of town that's exciting during the day may be dangerous at night.

A good travel agent and a few good travel books, plus some friends at home, may be able to give you solid information on your vacation city. They might tell you, for example, that you should use only police-licensed cabs, not the unlicensed type that exist in some cities. A ride in an unlicensed cab may be safe but it may not. Taking a ride in a gypsy cab, as they're called in New York City, is like hitchhiking—only you're paying for it.

Many people go to a city to have a good time and let off some steam. I'm not trying to be a spoilsport. I am trying to get you to go wherever you want with both eyes wide open. That includes talking with strangers. Common sense will tell you that you can't be both cautious and drinking heavily at the same time.

If you want to meet new friends, go places old friends recommend. Reliable travel books also have safe suggestions. If you want to hit the hot places in the seamy parts of town, beware!

There are thousands of con games designed to take your money. You know that nothing is free. Trust your instincts. If some idea or plan some new "friend" tells you about sounds too good to be true, it is too good to be true. Forget it. And him.

Have a good time on your vacation by leaving your house or apartment secure, by taking care of your valuables, and by taking good care of yourself.

8

Walking and Riding

Muggable Mary Glatzle again sat faking sleep on a bench. This time she was in the Bronx, on the perimeter of Crotona Park that borders on the broad Southern Boulevard. Nine undercover agents were close-by to protect her. She needed them.

Across the boulevard, some sixty yards from Mary and about the same from each other, stood two unmarked cars, their motors running, their occupants impatient. About a foot behind Mary's bench was a four-foot wall that held a sloping hill up into the park. Not far up the hill were three other policemen wearing assorted sloppy clothes. Two others sat on nearby benches.

Scarcely had Mary sat down with her pocketbook next to her left thigh than two men in straw hats stopped. In their early twenties, the two men looked her over, then quickly sat down on either side of her. The three men in the park were tense. So were the four in the two cars and the two on the benches. The men in the straw hats were huge and on both sides of her. This little woman might be in very big trouble.

But she wasn't. For some unknown reason, the straw-hatted men stood up and walked away without touching her or her pocketbook. You could see the officers relax. Mary, however, gave no outward sign of any emotion. She remained sitting up, with a mauve kerchief over her head, sunglasses covering her eyes, and a gray dress with white dots concealing a gun beneath.

Back across the street, Lieutenant Jim Motherway turned to his associate, Bob Lucente. "Look. Behind her, on that rock. Three kids. See them under the tree?"

It was hard to distinguish them. The streetlight was blocked by the tree but the white T-shirt of one teen-ager was visible. Seated in his car, Lieutenant Motherway had no communication with the three men in the park, but he knew they'd be as close to the kids and Mary as possible.

Catching three fast youths would be hard. They'd concentrate on the one who ran with the purse. Most important of all, Mary must be protected.

"Here comes one," said Lieutenant Motherway as the T-shirted youth came down from the rock to the wall. He looked at Mary, looked back to his comrades, then lay down on the top of the wall, right behind Mary.

"Here he goes," said the lieutenant as he fingered the lock on the door. It was unlocked. Bob, his driver, rubbed his palms on his pants, then put his hands on the wheel. The motor was still running. They were ready.

The kid's hand went down the wall and over the side of the bench. Down toward the pocketbook. But the hand stopped. The arm was too short; it couldn't reach the pocketbook!

Disgustedly, the kid got up off the wall and walked back to the rock under the tree. The teen-agers made another plan and they made it fast. All three came down to the wall and, for the first time, you could see that the youth in the T-shirt was much smaller than the other two.

Few people were walking past Mary this evening at about 8:30. Some did and paid no attention to her or to the teen-agers watching her. One man did. A tall thin fellow with a gray beard, he walked slowly past her, saw the three teen-agers, and shook his head. He didn't stop, he wouldn't stop, but he did shake his head as he walked away.

And then he looked across the street. He saw Lieutenant Motherway's unmarked car with the motor running. He looked back at Mary, at the teen-agers, then across at the car. He knew what was going on.

Now one of the kids got wise. He looked over, too. With a big smile on his face, he and the other two walked across the street right past the undercover car and went off.

"You can't win them all," said the lieutenant. "You win some and you lose some." What he didn't say was that you always do whatever you must to protect Mary. Even if that means being out in the open too much.

That three got away didn't make much difference. Two minutes later, Lieutenant Motherway said, "Here's a live one."

Walking down the street in a very neat suit was a man in his mid-twenties, his eyes on Mary. He stopped. He looked around not at people but for something. He found it on a bench to the right of Mary: some cardboard. He picked up the cardboard, carried it over to Mary's left side (where the pocketbook was), put down the cardboard, and sat down.

Lieutenant Motherway checked the lock on his door. Policeman Bob Lucente rubbed his palms on his pants and grabbed the wheel. "Watch his hand, watch his hand," said the lieutenant. Just then the man's left hand was kneading his right as he kept eying Mary and her open bag. He looked over and inside. He could see her wallet.

"There it goes, there it goes!" and the left hand was traveling over toward Mary, right for her pocketbook. The lieutenant checked the lock, the driver rubbed his palms on his pants, the man's hand went into the pocketbook . . . and came out with the wallet.

"Go!" yelled Lieutenant Motherway as Policeman Lucente shoved the car in drive and raced across the street against the sounds of screeching traffic.

Mary was up, her gun was out and pointed at the man. "Police. You're under arrest," she said.

"I didn't do anything," the man responded as he sat with her wallet in his lap.

The lieutenant's car and the second unmarked car roared across the street as the undercover agents from the park and the benches raced over. Handcuffs were put on the offender.

As the police went through his pockets, they found a very special knife: a weighted knife designed to fly point-first.

In the space of under thirty minutes in one section of one park of one New York City borough, six people had seriously considered or attempted or committed purse snatching from one woman.

As we drove the perpetrator back to the precinct station Lieutenant Motherway said, "For one or two weeks now, Southern Boulevard will be pretty safe. Word will get out that there are cops everywhere, dressed all kinds of ways. After that, we'll come back again."

You won't be asleep on a bench along Southern Boulevard now or two weeks from now. But you might be walking along it or along thousands of similar streets across the country, and there is some chance you will be mugged and your purse will be stolen. There is also a slight chance you will be raped.

Let's get specific. Larceny $50 and over includes only a portion of all instances of purse snatching and pick pocketing (as well as thefts of valuables from cars, which is discussed in Chapter 9). Yet FBI figures show more than 1.8 million offenses of larceny $50 and over last year, up 75 per cent since 1967. There were 374,560 instances of robbery reported (including muggings), up 85 per cent since 1967. And there were 46,430 forcible rapes (though this is only a percentage of all forcible rapes, for most are not reported), up 70 per cent since 1967. For larceny $50 and over there were 883 victims per 100,000 inhabitants, for robbery there were 180 victims per 100,000 inhabitants, and for forcible rape there were 43 victims per 100,000 inhabitants.

Some people read figures like these and become terribly afraid and filled with worry. Others react by thinking that their own chances of becoming a victim are very small so there's no threat to them.

No matter who you are or where you live or how you go about living, these figures are important to you because of one key insight by Sergeant Barbara Guarino of Los Angeles. In talking about street crimes, including purse snatching, mugging, and rape, Sergeant Guarino says, "The great majority of these crimes can be prevented. Most muggers, purse snatchers, and rapists act with the opportunity."

Don't be anxious and don't be carefree. Be realistic. Act to prevent becoming a victim and impress upon your loved ones the need for them also to act preventively. And, as Sergeant Guarino implies, the best way to act preventively is to do your best to eliminate the opportunity for crime to happen to you.

STREET CRIMES

There's a simple reason six would-be purse snatchers were attracted to Muggable Mary: she appeared to be asleep. As with burglars, these perpetrators of street crime look for an easy mark. They don't want to work hard and they don't want much risk of getting caught. So they go after women who are old and can't yell loud or put up any fight; they hit those who are drunk or tipsy or asleep or high on drugs; they rip-off those with canes or crutches.

If no elderly or incapacitated people are around, purse snatchers and muggers will attack women whose minds are a thousand miles away. During the day as well as at night, these teen-agers or cowardly men in their twenties and thirties or narcotics addicts are looking and waiting. Next time you're out walking, notice the other women. How many do you see who are completely wrapped up in some problem inside them or totally involved in a conversation or thoroughly engaged in getting from one place to another? In other words, how many women (and men) do you see who are not aware of the world around them?

Policewoman Joyce Holmes works undercover as a decoy for purse snatchers and muggers in a major East Coast city. "When I go out, I'm always prepared for something that might happen. Whether I'm alone or with friends, doing my work or personal things, if I've got any thinking to do, I do it before I go out of the house or the car. If I've got any problem, I get it sorted out before I go outside. That way I'm not thinking about any problem. I'm always alert. Most muggers won't hit people who look alert."

When you are walking during the day and talking with a friend or window shopping or hurrying to get from one place to another, remember to remain alert to the people and events around you. Don't be fearful, just be alert. Perhaps it will help if you think of your pocketbook not just as a bag but as a portable safe.

Distracting events are the setting for many purse snatchings. A fire, an accident, a police siren, or just a large number of people at a crosswalk are examples. So is bumping into you while he or a partner takes your wallet from your puse.

Carrying Purse in This Manner Assures Protection from Would-be Thieves.

NEVER Carry Your Purse in This Manner While Frequenting Crowded Areas!

Firmly Clasp Top Portion of Purse with Hand While Shopping, Riding or Standing in Crowded Buses, Streetcars . . . etc.

Courtesy of the San Francisco Police Department

The purse snatcher may be man or woman, sloppily or neatly dressed, may engage you in conversation (such as asking directions), or may come out of nowhere and run off in a second with your valuables. Once he's off, there's little chance of stopping him, catching him later, or getting your goods back.

So before you leave your house or apartment when you are going to do some walking, remind yourself that you must be alert to the possibility of crime. Think of this when you take hold of your pocketbook. It, not you, will be the object of most street crimes. Always carry your pocketbook close to your body, never let it dangle by its straps. If you have a shoulder bag, let it hang from your shoulder and keep an arm around it, don't dangle the straps from your hand. These positive actions are part of what Policewoman Holmes means when she says, "Be alert."

And before you leave your home, know where you're going. Just because you are familiar with an area doesn't mean it can't be dangerous. Although every city and town has some areas with more crime than others, criminals are just as mobile as anyone else. A mugger, or particularly a purse snatcher, can work in the most exclusive shopping areas without being suspected and without getting caught. Consider carrying your wallet in a coat pocket and not in your pocketbook.

Expensive jewelry, large amounts of money, or a careless attitude about credit cards can attract purse snatchers and muggers to you. Wear fine jewelry when you're going out with friends, not among crowds of people. And always be careful with money and credit cards. If possible, carry only what you think you'll need.

After you've been out and are returning home, approach your house or apartment-building entrance with your key out and ready to insert in the lock. Don't be looking for your key in your pocketbook, as you will be intent on finding the key and no longer alert.

Remember not to leave the key in the door, not even for a minute. It's a very bad habit. And don't put the key and your pocketbook down inside the open door while taking groceries into the kitchen or you'll be leaving your money and your home open to an outsider. Instead, place a small table near the door you enter carrying groceries. Upon entering, put the groceries on the table, remove the key, and double lock the door.

Women do less walking today than they used to because of the automobile and public transportation and because of the fear of crime. This is especially true at night. Yet young women, students, and working girls very often will walk during the day and even at night.

During the day, if a woman is walking on a sidewalk and thinks she's being followed, she need only cross the street. If a man follows, head for some people.

If walking and being followed by a car, simply turn around and walk back the other way. The car will have to turn around and will end up on the opposite side of the street.

If, while walking through a park or along a sidewalk or through a parking lot during the day, someone follows and talks to you, don't talk back. Any attempt to engage you in conversation or to catch your eye should be resisted. This, of course, is also true for the cat-calls of guys who stand in groups. If the person is following you and you don't want to put yourself out by turning around and walking the other way, turn to him and say, "Scram" or something similar. Keep it short and pointed, and then walk off.

If someone asks for directions, there's no harm in telling them the way if you keep your distance from them and are pretty sure all they really want is directions. If there's any question in your mind about their motivations, don't be friendly. If someone in a car asks for directions and you want to comply, remain several feet from the car. They'll be able to hear well enough and you'll be safe from a hand that might grab your purse or you.

Even during the day, it is better not to walk alone. If possible, walk with some friends. Just about everyone knows of the dangers in parks at night but, unfortunately, you must be extra alert in parks during the day, too. Try to enjoy parks with friends, not alone, and stay in areas with other people. Lovers won't appreciate that advice, nor will people who want to get off by themselves. But there are many different rip-offs occurring in our parks, and every once in a while there is the case history of someone like "Baby Doll."

Sergeant Barbara Guarino has worked decoy operations in Los Angeles. This statuesque redhead, with laughing eyes and a beautiful smile, becomes a little subdued when talking about Baby Doll, a rapist and a true sicko:

> We called him Baby Doll because he wore sheer baby-doll pajamas. He also wore garter belts and a Dodger baseball cap. A real weirdo, but vicious. He carried a butcher knife and would use it on a woman if she didn't submit.
>
> Most of his rapes occurred in Griffith Park, on a little-used path up to the Observatory. He'd hide behind bushes and wait for one or two women to come along. Sometimes he'd get

them during the day, sometimes he'd get them at night.

[Women would walk along this lonely path at night?] Yes, sometimes.

So we had to stop him. We had policemen in trees, behind distant bushes, at the bottom of the path, up near the Observatory, hidden just about anyplace a man could find. Then [Investigator] Connie [Davies] and I would walk up and down the path.

I don't know how many times we walked up and down that path. Over and over and over. The first few days, after we didn't have any luck, we thought he wouldn't show. Or maybe he had shown but he'd seen our men hiding.

Connie and I kept walking up and down that path one afternoon when there was a sound over to my side. Baby Doll was hiding behind a tree and was about to jump out at us when he saw an officer. He tried to get away but we caught him. Turned out Baby Doll was the son of a judge.

They call this type of rapist a "tree jumper." As you can imagine, there aren't many around who are that sick. But as much as you want to relax and enjoy yourself in a park, you also want to remain alert.

Muggers are also out day and night but in far greater numbers. They work alone or in pairs or groups, will attack anyone but prefer women, the elderly and the sick, and will always try to use the element of surprise.

While a pickpocket or purse snatcher doesn't intend to hurt you, a mugger might. He will use a weapon or his fist to threaten you or to hit you. He wants your money but he will trip you or hit you or beat you to get it.

Since the best way to surprise you is to get you from behind, that's what he'll do. He'll wait in a dark doorway until you've passed, then grab you. Or he'll walk toward you, size you up, walk past you, then turn around and grab you. (A large percentage of all muggings occur in hallways, basements, mailbox areas, and elevators, so be sure you've read Chapter 4 on Apartment Buildings.)

The best prevention is to walk briskly, alertly, and with self-confidence. Notice who is around you, notice what they're doing, and move on.

While pickpockets and purse snatchers work well in groups of people, muggers prefer solitary areas. So stay with or as close as possible to groups of people.

Even if you carry no pocketbook, a mugger might attack you. He'll think you have money in your pocket and, in most cases, he'd be right. So please don't think you needn't be cautious if you walk without a purse.

While a purse may attract the attention of a few, sexy clothing is designed to attract the attention of many. When you or your daughter are at a party with friends, provocative clothing may be appropriate. In the street, it is not. The clothes some young women wear may be everyday among their peers, but among others they can attract the wrong kind of attention.

All the policemen and the convicts (all men) I interviewed on the subject of sexy clothing had very definite views. One burglar, robber, and assaulter said, "I see a woman dressed sexy and I'm going to look. I'm going to say something, too. I mean, she's asking for it, isn't she?"

None of the convicts said he would attack a woman because she was dressed provocatively. Several policemen brought up the view that a man who wants some sex, either given willingly or forcefully, will think a woman in sexy clothes is interested.

Some policewomen agree up to a point. Says one, "A sexually dressed woman might get propositioned. Some guy might think she's a prostitute. But she *won't* get raped just because she's wearing those clothes."

You may have your own ideas on this subject and may very well want to dress any way you please. You'll be safer, however, if you always have a wrap of some sort to cover yourself. If you're going to a party, you may or may not plan to be out on the street. But you might go for a drink or to a late show or some other place where you would have to do some walking. So play it safe.

I don't know about you, but I'm very distressed that my wife can't go for a walk at night. I don't particularly like having to double lock the door every time I use it or keep all my windows secured or use a host of other crime-prevention measures. But restricting my wife's freedom to walk where she wants when she wants really upsets me.

But that's the way it is. Sometimes we'll go walking together, though we must be careful where we walk at night even if we are with a group of people. You already know you, too, must be careful.

I attended one meeting of the police and the community where an elderly woman asked, "Can't two women walk together at night without purses and be safe?"

The four officers, including one policewoman, all answered, "No." And the woman wasn't thinking of walking in a "bad" area; she wanted to walk in her own upper-class neighborhood. The difference between "bad" and "good" areas has diminished to the point that just about no areas at night are truly safe for women.

About the only safe way for a woman to walk alone or with another woman at night is described in this case history told to me by a young mother:

> I like to go out at night when it's dark and quiet and walk my dog. Sometimes I get bothered, though, like one time. Several guys pulled up in a car just as my dog went behind a bush. They were drunk and foul-talking but they didn't stay too long. My dog came out from behind the bush. They took one look at my Great Dane and drove off!

Some women, however, neither have nor want dogs yet want or need to be out walking at night. They need to get home from a bus or subway stop, to walk from work through a parking lot to the car, or they want to go to a drugstore, the corner market, a neighborhood movie theater, or visit a friend.

Sergeant Lee Kirkwood advises using a taxi whenever possible or delaying a trip to the Laundromat or store until daylight. "But if you must be out walking at night, know your route in advance. Know the restaurants and service stations that are open when you'll be walking by. Know the location of a pay phone or a police phone along your path, and determine beforehand if you know any neighbors who will be up when you're walking. In other words, *plan ahead*."

Here are some other tips from police departments around the country:

Go where there is light. If possible, avoid the dark.

Don't walk near dark buildings or high shrubbery or parked cars. People may be hiding in or behind these.

If there are no parked cars, walk near the curb and away from buildings. If cars are parked along the curb, walk in the center of the sidewalk.

If the sidewalk seems too dark or dangerous to walk on, walk in the center of the street.

Don't ever take shortcuts through alleys or parks at night and try to avoid sidewalks outside parks.

If at all possible, walk closely behind a group of nice-looking people. If you have to wait a few minutes for them, wait in a well-lighted area.

When you walk through a parking lot, have your keys out and ready to slip into your lock. Walk down the main aisles and stay in the light.

Do not be afraid to ask a friend to escort you to your car at night, or to meet you at your car and escort you to your apartment.

If someone in the distance is making you uncomfortable, look up to a light in a window and wave. Pretend someone is waiting up for you and is watching out for you.

The two keys of this list are *light* and *people*. Both mean safety for you. Darkness and being alone make you very vulnerable to attack by muggers and rapists.

A young, handsome, and mod New York detective has one last tip for you about walking at night:

> I worked the [Greenwich] Village for four years and investigated many rapes. Many rapes. And every time, the woman had a premonition. She had a feeling something bad was going to happen, but she thought she could beat it. She thought she could get into her apartment in time.
>
> Like one girl. Top of the block, she saw this guy. Her instincts told her to get away but she figured she was right near her home and she could make it. She walked fast but he got her.
>
> If you feel uneasy, call the police. Listen, we all like to take a few minutes to talk with a woman.

So if you must walk at night, know where the phones are along your route. Know the police phone number and have some dimes with you (unless the police in your area can be reached by dialing 911). You can also call the operator, but if there's a threat of trouble, call the police. Says Policewoman Cindy Miller, "The police would much rather escort you to your car or home than investigate a rape or a murder."

SUBWAYS, BUSES, AND CROWDS

Crowds attract pickpockets. Whether you're waiting to cross a street, get into a bus, or get out of a subway, you must be extracautious. The key: keep your mind on your money.

Your mind is not on your money if you are looking through your purse for a token as the bus or subway train approaches. Women who do that are vulnerable to purse snatching. Instead, have your token in hand before you leave your home or your work. That way your pocketbook will always be closed when you're on the street and you can remain alert.

If you're waiting for a subway train or a bus and you're getting crowded, a pickpocket may be at work. Three simple words will prevent a theft and give you some elbow room. The words: "Somebody's pushing me." Say this and everyone, including the pickpocket, will move back.

Whenever possible, wait for a bus and board it only from well-lighted areas. If the bus stop isn't flooded with light, complain to the transit authorities and, until they act, wait for the bus at a nearby store. Similarly, your safety is endangered if you get off a bus at a stop with inadequate light. Says Detective Larry Carr, "If you're going to a poorly lighted stop and have fears, don't get off there. Wait for a well-lighted stop, then take a taxi or have someone pick you up." Sometimes a bus driver will let you off at a bright area along his route even if it isn't a bus stop. If you're concerned, ask him.

While waiting for a subway train at night, you will be safer by remaining near the man in the change booth. If someone is following you or making you uncomfortable, go to him. "Just the appearance of talking to the man in the booth," says Detective Carr, "may scare off the follower. But if you want, you can have the man in the change booth call the transit police."

When the subway train comes, choose a car with several people in it. Avoid, if possible, the last car or any car with only one or two other passengers. If you are leery of someone, simply change your seat. Keep your eyes on the other passengers and, should you become disturbed by one of them, approach a transit officer and tell him.

The subway rides in some cities can be very long, especially at the end of the day. Some people close their eyes and some even fall asleep. Several women riding New York's IRT have fallen asleep and have been attacked right on the train—by the notorious "Kissing Bandit":

> Apparently hundreds of women have been kissed by a fleet-footed man as they sat asleep or with their eyes closed. A short kiss and then a fast run through the car always enabled his escape.
>
> Always, that is, until he added a new twist to his caper. One night he walked over to a woman who was asleep and kissed her. She thought she was just dreaming and kept her eyes closed. Then he bit her on the lip.
>
> The suspect fled one way as the victim ran screaming through the train the other way. She found a conductor who stopped the train and kept the doors closed until police arrived.
>
> The twenty-six-year-old suspect is now in custody.

AT WORK, IN STORES, IN THEATERS

Purse snatchers, other thieves, and even muggers keep their eyes open for opportunities in offices and factories, in ladies' rooms, department stores, dressing rooms, supermarkets, and parking lots. Keep your purse touching you physically at work or locked in a drawer (not just placed in a drawer) and keep it with you when you leave your work area.

When using the lavatory, keep your pocketbook right next to you. Don't leave it near or on the door where someone can grab it and run. Wear your jewelry when you're washing up. Don't take it off or you might turn around a moment later with clean hands but no ring or watch.

When making purchases in stores, if you cash a check or use a bill of large denomination and receive many dollars in change, you have told anyone interested that you have cash with you. If you feel uncomfortable carrying this cash, have someone from the store escort you to your car. Bundleboys in supermarkets can easily assist you and department stores will also give you a hand.

In movie theaters, both pickpockets and sex perverts are sometimes found. If you go to a theater alone, avoid dark corners and the rear seats of the first floor or balcony. Obviously you will avoid sitting near any potentially annoying man or teen-agers; try to sit near a family. If that's not possible, choose an aisle seat.

If you are annoyed by someone in a theater, a short expression of your feelings may stop him. If not, change seats or ask an usher for assistance. If the stranger persists and no usher is there to help, yell! Help will come very quickly.

Always keep your purse right on your lap, never on the seat next to you even if you put it under your coat. Pickpockets can get into your pocketbook and steal your wallet while you are absorbed in the movie, so keep your hands on your purse.

When changing clothes in a department store, don't hang your purse up with your clothes. Purse snatchers, male and female, hit people in even the most exclusive stores, as can be attested to by this wealthy woman:

> I had two outfits with me and was trying them on in the dressing room. I had just taken my own garments off when a hand reached over the door, grabbed my pocketbook, which was hanging on a door hook, and disappeared. I yelled and grabbed something to cover myself, but by the time I opened the door I could only see the back of a woman running away.
>
> Of course I immediately went to the management of [this very fine store]. They said they would conduct an immediate search and were confident they would have my purse and its contents back to me shortly.
>
> I went home and not half an hour later received a call from

the store. They had located my purse and asked me to come claim it. I was relieved.

But when I arrived at the store, they had not found my pocketbook and denied calling me. I was very puzzled until I returned home.

My furs, silverware, jewelry, several hundred dollars, two cameras, and other valuables were gone. I'd been burglarized!

The theft of your pocketbook can be only the beginning of your troubles. Some thief now has not only some of your valuables but the keys and address of your home. There are some cases of pickpockets mailing back a driver's license and other important papers and not bothering you again. But there are many cases of thieves entering a home with keys from a pocketbook and completely emptying the residence.

Your pocketbook is more than a portable safe. It literally contains the keys to your home. Safeguard it!

WIENIE WAVERS

When walking by a building or past a parked car or simply along a sidewalk, you may be confronted by a man committing indecent exposure. Laundromats, parking lots, and parks are also frequent stages for these perverted performances. In addition to the dirty old men who are usually depicted as the ones who commit this act, police records show doctors, lawyers, and other professional people who get their kicks this way. Sometimes these men are called "wienie wavers."

They won't harm you and there's no evidence that indecent exposure leads to any other crime. The man is sick and pathetic as he calls you to his car or opens up his coat so that you can see his genitals. He wants to shock you for that's the way he gets his charge.

Investigator Connie Davies, a tall and attractive mother of two who has worked as a decoy to catch rapists, has attempted to catch some wienie wavers. The following is one of her best histories:

> I had one case of a man, married with two kids, who would expose himself on the golf course. He always chose the third

green, right near a wooded area of one course. He'd wear regular jeans but underneath would have on his wife's golden bikini bottoms. He liked these the best not because they were golden but because they had draw strings at both sides. He could pull both strings and, whoops, there he was!

We received several complaints so we staked out the third green. I was trying to play golf. Many times on many different days, I was hacking away while other officers were watching for him. He never showed up while I was there.

Some other officers caught him, though, right on that third green. He'd done his thing for some women golfers and we caught him. I followed up the case, talking with women who'd filed complaints and found one who was so shocked by this wienie waver that it improved her golf game.

[Wait a minute, please. Did you say she was so shocked her golf game improved?] Yes. That's what she told me. From then on, she says she kept her head down and her eyes on the golf ball.

In addition to the obvious problems relating to wienie wavers, there is one more: the police have a tough time catching these men because women are seldom able to identify them. Why? Because women don't look at the wienie waver's face.

This is what happens: the man confronts a woman, she sees what he's about and is shocked, so she stomps off.

It is a shocking experience. An adult man is showing how infantile he can be. He is a nuisance to society and, very often, a source of guilt and bafflement to himself. He needs psychological help.

What the police need is the description and, if he exposes himself in his car, his license-plate number. In the event that you should meet a wienie waver, remember what the police want and try to provide it.

9

Driving

As with all of the other chapters, although some of the discussion concerns things like pocketbooks and lights and locks and homes, the main subject is you. That's who the police and I and you want to protect, you and your loved ones.

Auto thefts are a big problem in our country. Last year almost one million (881,000 to be exact) were reported stolen. That's one every thirty-six seconds, one out of every one hundred and nine registered cars. You already have auto theft insurance, but that seldom covers your entire loss or your inconvenience, or the price of goods stolen from within your car. Nor does insurance soothe the national pains of youths whose first crime is joy-riding in a stolen car.

And most importantly, someone can get into your car when you are not there, can stay there and wait for you, or can get in when you are already inside.

Your car can lead you out of danger, or into it. A breakdown can make a woman open for harm just as a lack of knowledge of the ways some perverts operate can lead to sexual attacks.

The best answer is prevention: prevention of theft, of breakdown, and of unwanted entry.

Thefts of bicycles and of boats are rising so I have included some material on these two subjects at the end of the chapter.

AUTO THEFT

Your car is not just a piece of mechanical equipment, it is your home on wheels. Many women spend hundreds and hundreds of hours a year in their cars. Since that's where you sometimes are, that's where you must be protected always.

Betty and Bob are a lively, outgoing couple in their early thirties who live in a small, two-bedroom suburban home. Like most of us, they are not always careful with their keys. Betty is the speaker:

>I was coming home from shopping on a Tuesday afternoon and I was late so I left the car key in the ignition, took out the house key, and ran inside. I put my two bundles down, ran out, and got the rest. I left the motor running because I had one more errand to do and, besides, it would take only a minute to put away the milk and cheese and things.
>
>So I got everything put away and dashed out of the house for the car but it wasn't there!
>
>I took only a minute and I was awfully upset as I looked up and down the street. I called Bob and the police and they started a search for it.
>
>Three days later, the car suddenly appeared in the driveway. I just happened to look out the window and there it was. I ran out and found a little note on the windshield. It said, "Sorry I took your car but needed it for an emergency. Please forgive the inconvenience. Hope you can use these." And there were two baseball tickets enclosed.
>
>Well, Bob and I guessed it wasn't so bad. We called the police, told them the car was back, and, a few days later, went off to the baseball game.
>
>When we came home, there wasn't a piece of furniture in the house. The built-in stove was just about the only thing left!

None of the neighbors heard the burglars move anything out of Bob and Betty's home so now the young couple have a car, a built-in stove, and some insurance money to start refurnishing their home. The first thing they did was to make each other some promises. Says Betty, "We vowed never to leave keys in the car again, never to leave the motor running, and never to leave the car unlocked." I asked them if, in the two months since the auto theft and burglary, they had kept these promises. They both answered, "Yes."

The chances are the young mother in the following case history has made similar promises. I didn't meet her but the police are pretty sure she's learned her lesson:

A car pulled up outside a drugstore and the driver, a young woman, rushed out. Leaving the car running, she raced into the pharmacy with the prescription for a much-needed medication.

Two young boys, witnesses said they were about thirteen or fourteen, were walking along near the drugstore when they spotted this car. They looked at each other and the excitement in their eyes said, "Let's do it!"

They did it. The taller boy sat behind the wheel as they both got in and zoomed away.

They hadn't gone more than two blocks, however, when they heard a noise in the back seat. For the first time, they looked around. Behind them was a baby.

Police found the vehicle moments later. The doors were open, the blinker light was on, and the car was standing in the middle of a street. Apparently the young thieves had liked the idea of joy-riding but not of kidnaping.

It may be hard for you to imagine how a mother can leave her car running with a baby inside, but it is also hard for the police to understand how so many people can leave their keys in the car and the car unlocked. Even without a baby inside, your car is one of your most expensive possessions. Would you leave $1,000 or $2,000 or $3,000 in cash out in the street? Of course not. But that's what people do when they leave keys in the car, or take their keys but leave the car unlocked.

National figures show that 80 per cent of stolen cars have been left unlocked and 42 per cent had the key in the ignition.

So the first steps in preventing the theft of your car are always to take your key with you and always lock your car and roll up your windows. Sometimes you'll be away from the car only a minute and sometimes you'll be parking your car behind your apartment or in your garage. In these situations, as well as all others, take your keys with you and lock the car. Even when it's parked in your own garage. There's no other safe way.

Leaving a key in the car visor or under the seat is a bad idea. So is hiding the key on the outside of the car. As with a house key, thieves know all the hiding places, so don't secret a key someplace outside your house or car. You might want to leave an extra car key with a neighbor or in a safe place at work.

What about parking attendants who want you to leave the key in the car? Do your best to avoid them. Many parking lots require people to leave keys in the car, tell you they're not responsible for your car, and charge you if you don't leave the keys. Unless you absolutely must, don't stand for this foolishness. Find another lot where you don't have to leave your keys.

But if you must leave your keys, leave only the ignition key. Never the trunk key, never your house, office, or any other keys. Says one New York detective, "It's not always a guy running around with a Celluloid strip who breaks into your home. Sometimes it's a guy with a key. Never give your house key to a parking attendant, for he can check your license number and, through devious means, get your address. Then he can make an impression of your key and go in anytime he wants."

If it is frequently necessary to leave your ignition key when parking the car with an attendant, it's more convenient to have a key chain that makes it easy to separate the ignition key from the others. It's also safer, as you won't be tempted to leave all the keys.

Car accessories and other valuables are frequently stolen from cars. You have almost no chance of getting stolen accessories back unless you engrave your driver's license number (or social security number) on them. (This is the Operation Identification method described in Chapter 6.) Other items should not be left in your car even if they're not very valuable. A thief doesn't know that a brown bag inside your car contains dog biscuits. He may think it's something he can use.

Sam, a thief in his late thirties who wouldn't say much to me, did tell me about stealing from cars:

> I go by a car parked along the street. I see there's valuables inside, a package or something. Bam, I take it.
> They leave valuables inside the car, I'm going to take them. It's cold. It's simple.

It's also very true. Keep valuables in the trunk and put them there just before you drive away, not when you stop and park. For example, if you enter your car with a new lamp and know you're going to make a stop before home, put the lamp in the trunk before you start the car. If you put the lamp in the trunk after you've stopped the car, someone might see this and pry open your trunk while you're about your business. Similarly, if you're driving and it becomes so warm you no longer want to wear a coat, don't leave the garment in the car and don't put it in the trunk when you stop. Take it with you.

Thieves sometimes will break into a car to get valuables from the glove compartment. That's why the glove compartment should have only copies of important papers, if necessary, and not the papers themselves. If state laws don't require that facsimiles of the registration papers be in the auto, leave them in a bank vault. The lock on your glove compartment might keep a ten-year-old out, but don't count on it.

Door locks are none too reliable, either. Most car thieves don't pick these locks. Either the doors are open or the thief can get a tool inside the car to open the lock. Manny is an experienced car thief. "There isn't a car I can't get into," he proclaims, though there also isn't a policeman who can't catch him. The way he tells it, he's been in jails and prisons more times than you've put keys in a lock. A big man, he's about six-foot-three and over two hundred pounds. I asked him the best ways to prevent auto theft:

> Easy. Lock the car and take the keys. That's how. Almost every car I ever stole had keys in it or was unlocked.
> And another thing. An alarm. Those things are hard to saw through, those alarm cables. They've got something on them and they're hard to saw through. If you don't know there's an

alarm and you open the car and it starts ringing, you get
scared. You run.

[Do people pay attention to a car with the alarm ringing?]
Oh, no. They're not going to grab me, if that's what you
mean. No. But it sure as hell scares a guy who's breaking into
it. He wants to get out of there. He runs.

Since two thirds of all auto thefts occur at night and over one half
are from private residences, apartments, or residential streets, auto
alarms are helpful. They can alert you that your car is being tam-
pered with as well as scare away the potential thief.

While newer cars have lockable steering columns as standard
equipment, manufacturers are now offering optional alarm systems
on some models. In a few years, these factory-installed alarm systems may also be standard. But a few years from now won't help
you today, especially since newer cars are *not* most frequently stolen.
Chevrolets, Fords, and Volkswagens of all years are very popular
with auto thieves, but it is seven- and eight-year-old cars that are
most often taken. The youths want them for fun, for souping up, and
for parts. The pros go after newer cars.

The auto manufacturers are supplying alarm systems that blow
the horn and flash the lights. Better than that are alarms that ring
bells or activate sirens. Bells and sirens attract more attention than
horns and are more apt to deter thievery. Reliable alarm systems
cost between $50 and $100 installed and cover the doors, the hood,
and the trunk. Systems utilizing your horn cost a little less than bell
alarms while sirens cost the most (and may not be legal in your
state). Get information and estimates from several sources before
making a decision.

When you put in your auto-alarm system, you'll be given a decal
warning all to its presence. Some policemen and car thieves say the
decal is a deterrent, telling some would-be criminals to move on to
an easier target. Other experts say that surprise is the best deterrent.
Additionally, a professional thief may know how to disengage your
alarm, so these experts say you shouldn't use your alarm decal.

I think you should display your alarm decal. The great majority
of auto thieves (72 per cent) are under twenty-one, and looking for
a car that's easy to steal. And many of the pros, like Manny, don't

know how to disconnect the alarm. If you display your decal, it seems to me you'll have a better chance of deterring this crime.

The alarm is a deterrent, the locking steering column is a disabling device. Other disabling devices you might consider are secret ignition switches and secret gas-line shutoffs that must be activated before the car will start. Also available are push-button anti-theft ignition systems. Even if the key is in the ignition, the buttons on this system must be pushed in the right combination or the car won't start.

PROTECTING YOURSELF

There are many ingenious devices to deter car theft. Depending upon how much crime there is where you park and drive your car, you might need the protection offered by this equipment. But wherever you park and drive your car, you will have to rely on yourself to deter some crimes. Electronic equipment and other devices help only so far, then you must act for yourself.

Far too many women who drive, however, have a problem: they are afraid of cars. Even if it is their own car, these women think that cars belong to men, cars are something only men know about. While other women are taking courses in auto mechanics at adult education programs and automobile clubs, these women turn to their man to find out if there's enough gas in the car.

The great majority of men know very little about automobiles and there is usually no need for anyone to know more than a few fundamentals. The point is that your car can leave you stranded in a dangerous situation. You want to prevent that. Says Sergeant Kirkwood of Los Angeles, "It is not safe for a woman who drives to be ignorant about her car."

The car you use should be maintained according to the schedule set down by the manufacturer. A booklet in the glove compartment gives this schedule and also offers an introduction to the workings of the car. Read the booklet and learn something new about your car. Know, for example, exactly what the various gauges monitor and what to do if one of them shows that there is a problem.

Next time you pull into a gas station, ask the attendant to check the oil, water, battery, and tires. Watch him as he checks these fundamental components and learn the proper levels of them all (the glove compartment or a front door lists the proper tire pressure). When you see your tires at the proper inflation, you will always be able to give them an eyeball check before getting in your car. You won't want to be riding on over- or underinflated tires. Nor do you want to drive a car with tires that may blow. At least once a week, look at your tires, checking for nails, glass, gouges, and tread wear.

Everytime, before you drive away, check the gas level. Make this a habit. One of the most common causes of car breakdowns is running out of gas. Make it a habit to check your gauge every time you start up. Also, learn how far you can go on a quarter tank of gas. You can ask the gas station attendant or your man, but the best way to find out is to do it yourself. Note the mileage when the car is full of gas, then when it's three-quarters full. When you know your number of miles per quarter tank, subtract a few miles to allow for such variables as bad weather, heavy traffic, or city driving as opposed to highway travel.

Always approach your car with your keys out, ready to unlock your doors. Day or night, this is a simple and excellent security habit. If possible, always park in well-lighted areas. When you park during the day and know you won't return to the car until after dark, try to determine which areas will have good light. Before you park, also check for loiterers. They will sometimes break into cars even if the area is flooded with light.

Before getting into your car, another good security habit is to check the floor behind the back seat. You will need a flashlight to do this at night so carry a small one with you. Police all over the country recommend this precautionary measure to ensure that you don't get in the front while a man is hiding in back.

After backing out of your garage, it is always safest to lock your garage door. This deters a stranger from entering your garage and waiting for your return.

When driving it is best to travel on familiar, well-lighted streets that are busy with auto and pedestrian traffic. When this isn't possible, be extra alert. Shortcuts through unfamiliar areas may actually take longer. If you become lost, it may be unwise to ask a pedestrian for directions. Instead ask a policeman or stop at a well-lighted service station.

Light again is your friend when you stop at night for something to eat or for gas. Try to find a restaurant parking lot or service station that has plenty of light.

Every time you drive, day or night, all your doors should be locked and your windows, all of them, should be closed. If it's hot and you need some ventilation, have one or two windows open only an inch, and use the car blower. Never have windows open so much that a hand can come in.

Most often, the hand that comes in will be coming for a pocketbook or other valuables placed on the seat beside you. So place no valuables near you (or on the seat behind you). Keep things out of sight on the floor.

Bus stops, traffic lights, and stop signs are favorite hangouts for purse snatchers. They may mingle with people at the corner of the street but will lunge for the pocketbook of an unsuspecting woman if her window is down or her door unlocked.

Rapists also loiter near intersections. Sergeant Genevieve Hauck is a twenty-five-year veteran of the Los Angeles Police Department. Among the multitude of cases that she's handled is the following:

> The suspect would wait at a traffic light. When the signal caused cars to stop, he'd look them over. He wanted a woman driver with an unlocked driver door. If he spotted one, he'd start across the crosswalk, then open the woman's door, push her across the seat, and drive off.
>
> This is not an isolated case. We've had several cases of this type, some were robbers, others were rapists.
>
> The particular man I was thinking about when we started talking was a rapist. We caught him. We had a policewoman decoy as a driver and a policeman crouched down behind the seat.

Sometimes women who are alone when they drive will be followed. Whether the followers are drunk troublemakers who are "just looking" or a man who intends to assault you, there's one place you should not go. That's home. To bring such a person home is to

show him where you live so he can come back again to bother you
and your family. Worse yet, he might attack you before you actually
get into your home.

Madeleine is the mother of two children and an attractive social
worker in her late twenties. She has a great sense of humor but can
be strong when she has to. Recently, she had to:

> I was driving home from my office and I was quite tired. It
> had been a busy day. The car was a quiet refuge between
> work and the kids, and my mind was just relaxing. Of course
> I was watching the traffic ahead of me but I wasn't watching
> behind me. A car was following me right to my home.
>
> Since I didn't see this guy, I arrived home and parked in
> the street where I usually do. My mind was just picking up as
> I started to the apartment. Then this hand came from out of
> nowhere.
>
> It was pretty dark and I couldn't see his face very well but
> I knew instinctively what was going on, and I wasn't having
> any of it. He grabbed my shoulder and started to pull me
> toward his car. I started screaming and kicking and hitting and
> biting and I don't know what else. He released his grip and
> jumped back in his car. He drove off. I was okay.

The best place to lead someone following you is a police station.
That'll scare him! When that's not possible, however, drive into a
service station. If you want to get some fast action, drive into a
service station with your horn blaring intermittently. Heads will turn
and so will the car following you. Drive-in restaurants are almost as
good as service stations. If you can get the man's license-plate number, copy it down and phone the police. Even if you can't get the
number, contact the police and give them all the information you
can. They'll have cars patrolling the area to catch him.

When you're driving, the only one who can legally force you to
stop is a policeman. A private citizen can motion you to slow down
for an accident or an obstacle in the road, but no one other than an
officer can make you stop. If you come across an accident and want
to help, often the best thing you can do is find out what's wrong and
drive to the nearest safe place to telephone.

There is one situation in which you must pull over to the side of the road and stop, and another situation in which you might be tempted to do this. Investigator Connie Davies of Los Angeles talks about both:

> When you get involved in an accident, you must pull over. The law says that you must exchange information on your car insurance with the other driver and you must call the police if damage is over $200. But no woman needs to get out of her car to exchange this information. She can roll down her window a little and pass it out. We have had cases of men who purposely caused minor accidents with women drivers to stop them. When the women would open their doors, the men would attack them.
>
> We have also had cases of men who cruise the boulevards and freeways at night looking for women alone at the wheel. When the suspect would find a woman, he'd flash his headlights, beep his horn, and point to a rear tire to get the woman to pull over. If she did, he'd walk to her car and tell her, "Your wheel is coming off. You'd better get out." When the door opens, he's in.
>
> The most recent man to pull this rear-wheel scam [or illegal scheme] is a twenty-nine-year-old who violently beat up his victims, raped them, forced oral copulation, and robbed them. He's a married man with two children.

Your car door is like your front door. You never want to open it unless you're sure who's on the other side. If you're unsure, roll the window down just an inch and carry on any necessary conversation.

AUTO BREAKDOWNS

If another motorist should motion to you that you have some sort of car trouble, it is best not to pull over at the side of the road, whether that road is a highway or a street in the city, suburbs, or countryside. Instead, try to make it to a service station. Policewoman Paula James gives self-protection lectures to the public. "Maneuver into the slow or breakdown lane," says Policewoman James, "and drive slowly to a gas station. That may mean exiting the freeway or it may mean driving a few miles. It may also mean ruining a tire or some other part of the car. But a woman alone, especially at night, should do everything possible to avoid being stranded."

If you just can't make it to a service station, a busy intersection is your second-best objective.

And if you find it impossible to do anything but pull over to the side of the road and stop, then be sure to stay with your car. To walk off down the road or hitchhike for help is to invite trouble. The distress signals known all over the country are a raised hood (Do you know how to raise the hood of your car?) and a white handkerchief tied on the antenna or the driver's door handle. Emergency flashers can also be used.

Some heavily traveled highways near major cities have emergency phones stationed every quarter of a mile. If you are able to get your car right up to one of these phones, use it. But if you have to walk any distance to get to this phone, stay in your car.

As a matter of fact, some police experts suggest that, as long as the disabled car is safely off the road, the lone woman should give no distress signal. She shouldn't get out of her car to raise the hood or put out a white handkerchief or even simply put on the car's emergency flasher. Says Sergeant Kirkwood, "A stranded car with a woman inside can attract the wrong attention." Instead of using a distress signal, the driver should keep an eye out for a police car, then put on the flashers and beep like crazy when it comes close.

So whatever type of street or highway you're stranded on, the safest procedure is to sit tight with no outward sign of car trouble and wait for help to come by. Before the police drive by, however, a car may stop and the driver may ask if he can help. Since you won't know the person, your safest response is to roll down your window an inch, give him a dime, and ask him to make a phone call. You don't want him to check the engine, change the tire or whatever. You want him to call the police or an authorized towing service.

If someone stops who bothers you or makes you feel uncomfortable and you don't want his help at all, simply tell him, "Thank you but I already have help on the way."

A dark city street or a lonely highway at night might have no police cars patrolling for hours at a time. The driver of a disabled car may have to spend the entire night sitting tight, waiting for daylight to walk to a phone. But your car is far safer than a lonely street at night. According to Sergeant Kirkwood, "Few assailants will break a car window to get in."

It may seem odd to you that a man who would rape a woman wouldn't break a car window. It also may seem more fearful to spend a night in a car on a road than to have a stranger change a tire. And it may seem overly suspicious to refrain from displaying any of the usual distress signals.

You are safest if you follow the advice of the police. If you decide to take some risks, then you may have to pay the consequences.

There are two last points I'd like to mention about auto breakdowns. The first is common sense: drive with someone else as much as possible. Don't drive alone or with just your children whenever you can have another adult, male or female, with you. The second suggestion was mentioned to me by a convicted armed robber. This very intense man says, "Every man and woman should have a CB radio in their car."

It's a great idea for those with over $100 to spend. The CB radio is a Citizens Band two-way radio. You can get them for your home, office, and most important to this discussion, your car. A new program called Highway Emergency Locating Plan (HELP) is being promoted by auto clubs and other groups to help motorists equipped with this two-way radio. Channel 9 on the CB band is continuously monitored by private citizens, police, road service stations, and hospital emergency rooms. A stranded motorist sends out a call for help and it's soon on the way.

An FCC license is needed before you can transmit with CB equipment but the license is easy to obtain. You need no technical knowledge. You do need to be a United States citizen, eighteen years or older, and have $8.00. The simplest mobile units cost about $100 installed in your car and are available at many stores that sell standard radios and electronic equipment.

BICYCLES

Bicycle sales are booming and so are bicycle thefts. Many buyers and most thieves prefer the new ten-speed models by Schwinn,

Peugeot, and others. These are the "in" bikes with ecology- and health-minded cyclists.

There are two things to do if you want to prevent your bike from being stolen. First, forgo a new model and choose a used bike. It may be just as good as a new one and it won't be as desirable to a thief. Secondly, a strong bicycle padlock is the best device to secure your bike. If you want to use a chain, however, you want it to be at least 5/16-inch hardened-steel alloy and of continuous welded construction. Bolt cutters will do a job on anything less. Whenever possible, secure your bike to a bike rack or other heavy object. If you keep your bike in a garage, secure it into a $3/8 \times 6$-inch screw that's fastened into a stud.

Most of the bike thieves are in their teens and use hit-and-run tactics to gain pocket money. Some are college students who organize groups that steal from one campus, pile the bikes into a van, and sell them on another campus. While some thieves take only unlocked bikes, many do use bolt cutters.

Stolen bikes have only about a 3 per cent chance of being returned unless they are registered. Registered, licensed bicycles with identifying marks etched into the frame have about a 50 per cent chance of being returned. Your city or town may register bikes, but unless the entire state requires it and has a central office handling the information and theft reports, the action taken is not effective enough.

And even in the best of circumstances, getting back a stolen bicycle is a hassle. Keep bikes locked with a padlock at school, outside the home, in the garage, at a friend's—every place—and you stand a better chance of keeping your bike.

BOATS

The prevention of boat theft is of importance to the growing number of women who own boats. Protection of a boat combines crime-prevention measures for protecting homes and cars plus some measures that are special.

On cabin-type vessels, as with your home, have sturdy locks for windows, portholes, doors, and hatches. Have curtains or blinds that obscure views of the interior. For any boat, have an inventory list of all valuables, etch identifying marks on all portable gear and record this number plus serial numbers on the inventory list. When leaving your boat unattended for an extended period, store all portable valuables in a secure place ashore. Also consider installing an audible burglar alarm.

As is best at home, cooperate with your boating neighbors. Watch his property during his absence and ask him to watch yours. Note the description of unauthorized persons and boats loitering in the vicinity of docks and moorings.

Similar to your car, mechanically propelled vessels are to be registered with your state. Since this registration system helps prevent theft and helps in the return of stolen boats, consider registering your boat even if it is not mechanically propelled. All registered vessels must display their numbers on the hull. As you won't keep your car registration certificate in the glove compartment (keep a duplicate, if state law allows), your boat registration certificate also should not be left aboard, especially if the boat is unattended. To make the theft of your boat difficult, you can equip your ignition system with a secret cut-off switch or you can remove the rotor from the distributor.

To prepare for the chance that your registration numbers might be removed or obliterated, place these numbers on a principal timber or member of the hull. Secure your outboard motor to the boat by using a strong padlock (see Chapter 2) and chain (see under Bicycles just above). When storing your boat at a mooring, use a similar lock and chain in addition to your mooring line.

The above information is adapted from New York Police Department materials. The police also want you to inform them of people attempting to sell marine equipment at prices below the reasonable market value. And, in the event of boat or equipment theft, notify authorities immediately and have your inventory list available for them.

10

Confrontation with a Mugger or Rapist

It happened about three years ago. I was twenty. I was walking home from a girl friend's at nine o'clock at night. It was just two blocks and I was eating potato chips. I was on a small street and about to cross when I heard footsteps behind me. They had to come from the bushes. I knew that area. I was afraid to turn around and hoped he wouldn't bother me.

He came up to me. He had a knife. I tried to scream but no sound came out. He didn't look rough, he was even good-looking. He asked for money, but I think he asked for money mostly to calm me.

Things aren't too clear in my mind. I was very scared way down deep but I wasn't too scared, if that makes any sense. He held me with one hand and kept the knife against my side. We walked across the street.

The houses all had fences and the first three gates were locked. Then he found an open gate and shoved me through it. We went around back.

He told me to take off my clothes but I wouldn't. He started to unzip my dress but I told him, "Stop it."

He started touching me and I told him, "Stop it." I told him, "I'm pregnant." He felt my stomach and said I didn't feel pregnant. I told him I was and he stopped touching me.

He pulled out his thing and kept shoving it in my mouth. I kept spitting it out. Pretty soon he shot all over the place, then told me not to make a sound for five minutes and disappeared. I started to cry. I was more scared now than before. I ran to a house, banged on the door, and the man and woman let me in but they didn't believe me. Not at first, but then they did.

We called the police and the man went out looking for him. The man didn't find him but several months later the police did. I saw him in court after he had raped several women including a twelve-year-old girl. He wasn't rough with me but he was with some others. When I saw him in court he was with his girl friend. She was beautiful and didn't believe he could do anything bad.

The young woman who told me this case history, call her Judy, is now married to a policeman. She knows some women who have been raped and have had to seek extensive psychiatric treatment. She knows other rape victims who have gone on to lead healthy, normal lives. Judy was not actually raped but she does have some scars. She never walks anywhere at night. She is afraid to walk down even her own street during the day and, wherever she is, she never likes to have anyone behind her.

The majority of murders, aggravated assaults, and rapes occur not between strangers but between people who know each other. These crimes will be discussed in Chapter 13. Most women I have talked with, however, are afraid of being physically or sexually assaulted by strangers. These assaults, motivated by money or sex, are the subject of this chapter.

"What do muggers and rapists look like?" is a question many people have. Policewoman Cindy Miller says, "You can never tell just by someone's looks whether or not he's going to give you trouble." Muggers and rapists have no distinguishing features. There are cases of rapists who are homely, others who are handsome, some who dress neatly, others who are slobs or weirdo in appearance. Some seem to have normal relationships with a wife or girl friend and there are those who have no relationship with anyone. While you can see sickness in the eyes of the truly crazy men, certain drugs and sometimes just alcohol makes some people act crazy. Two thirds (63 per cent) of arrested rapists are under twenty-five, almost half (49 per cent) are black, and almost half (49 per cent) are white.

Policewoman Cindy Miller, who works undercover vice operations in Los Angeles, has some advice for all women:

> A woman who never even thought about being mugged or raped would be in great trouble if it happened. If a woman just one time thinks, "What if a man attacked me?" if she just thought about it one time, she'd be much safer. Just so that she has something to fall back on.
>
> If you've thought about it before, your thought will flash into your mind. If you haven't thought about it before, nothing will come to mind and you'll do nothing or you'll panic.

Policewoman Miller and her associates use the "What if . . . ?" technique to help prepare themselves for the unexpected. There are a few general rules about confrontations with robbers and rapists that are more often true than not:

> The best defense is prevention.
>
> During a confrontation, your objective is escape. Fight only if necessary.
>
> Use the minimum amount of force necessary. Screaming, breaking a window, or just shoving the offender may stop some confrontations.
>
> If the man has a weapon, do not start off fighting or he may use it on you.
>
> If you're fighting for your life, fight dirty.

So much for general rules for, as Sergeant Genevieve Hauck notes, "Each circumstance is different. You can't just set down some rules. You've got to be alert."

"What if I'm asleep and I wake up to find a strange man in my room and he's coming toward me? He's unarmed."

The first thing in your mind must always be escape. You really don't want to fight with any man since he'll probably win. To escape from a bedroom you must first get free of the covers. Throw the covers off.

Then scream. Screaming is one of the best weapons you have. Some loud screams will scare him and will alert others.

You can also alert others by breaking a window or by smashing a vase or lamp on the floor. Vases, lamps, anything that can do damage to him can also be used in your own defense.

"But can't he choke me?"

Some rapists are delighted when women fight back. Fighting back always runs the risk that he will beat you up or choke you. On the other hand, there is a chance that screaming and fighting and making noise will scare him away.

A key point to remember is that a mugger or a rapist does not expect a woman to fight back. He expects her to give in. Whether or not you should fight depends upon you, the assailant, the particular circumstances, and what you think your chances are of escaping. Above all, you want to avoid panic. Panic paralyzes you.

"Try to prepare yourself for an attack in your bedroom by looking around the room now and seeing what you can use to break a window, to defend yourself, or, better yet, how you can escape through a door or window." So says Sergeant Barbara Guarino.

There are some burglars who don't plan to rape but, once inside the home, they see a woman and attack her. Very often, however, the burglar-rapist has convinced himself that the woman actually wants to have sex with him.

This is a common attitude among rapists who act on impulse. Saying that you don't or making half-hearted gestures to escape won't change his mind. You must either make noise that brings help or get out.

"What if he's armed?"

Then you've got to determine if you're fighting for your life or your principles. If you're not fighting for your life, you are the only one who can decide if you want to submit or fight. If you fight, you may escape or you may end up raped and beaten, perhaps dead.

"Most sexual attacks are accompanied by little physical harm," says Dr. Robert Alan Cole, a psychiatrist in Los Angeles who works with sex offenders. "A man who commits aggressive rape often feels a tension building up inside of him. At his worst point of tension, the man may border on the psychotic. In fact, for a few instants he may be psychotic."

The following case history concerns M.R., an aggressive rapist who usually attacked women in the streets. He was caught, served time in prison, and is now on parole as well as seeing a psychiatrist:

> I used to get this feeling building up in me. I'd fight with my wife or get fired from a job or I'd get really pissed off at something and I'd be, you know, frustrated. Really frustrated, and angry.
>
> This feeling would build and build way up. But I mean *way* up, like I was going to explode if I didn't find a way to get it out. Sometimes I'd start drinking or taking pills but that wouldn't do it. I'd have to find a way to get it out. It just kept building.
>
> So I'd find some woman. I'd drive along looking for some woman walking at night. I'd explode if I didn't do it so I'd do it. Then I'd feel better.

M.R. exemplifies the psychotic behavior Dr. Cole is talking about. Dr. Cole continues, "After he has found relief, he leaves his victim and returns to a state approaching normal behavior."

You will have to judge the mental state of the armed man in your bedroom. He may be plain crazy. He may be so high on drugs or alcohol that he's the same as crazy. He may not hear a word you say because he's so far off in his own world. Or he may expect to attack you in your sleep and be scared off by your scream.

M.R. is a quiet man in his late thirties, of average height and quite strong, with a craggy, masculine face. He has been under intensive psychiatric care and has yielded to treatment. Here's what he suggests:

> [How can a woman prevent being raped?] I don't know. Don't be outside where you can get hurt, I guess. But one thing's for sure, a woman doesn't want to start screaming when a guy has a knife. No way. Scream and he'll stick you, he'll panic and stick you.

[So what should she do?] Well, I guess she could pretend she was too afraid to scream. Maybe she could pretend that way then catch him off guard or something a minute later.

After these many different answers, let's repeat the question. "What if I'm asleep and I wake up to find a strange man in my room coming toward me, and he's armed?"

Investigator Connie Davies has the best answer I've heard: "Scream, hit him, knee him, but when rape is inevitable, give in. Most people who end up in the hospital or are murdered after a rape have fought back when they haven't had a chance. Don't try any more, don't fight any more when rape is inevitable or he'll beat you to a pulp or kill you."

"What if I'm stopped at a traffic light and someone tries to get into my car?"

Beep the horn. An intermittent beeping is better than a long beep because the latter may just mean the horn is stuck. So beep that horn and, if the intersection is clear, go. As long as you won't cause an accident, drive through the red light. If you're very lucky, you might even attract a policeman.

"What if my car breaks down and I let someone inside to help but, instead, he attacks me?"

Scream, yell, put on the interior light, beep the horn, break a window. Attract attention through sound and light.

Sergeant Barbara Guarino, plus other policemen and policewomen, has observed that "a woman in danger is very strong." As long as this attacker has no gun, knife, or other weapon, fight him off. You may want to get out of the car but, in most circumstances at night, that could lead to more trouble. Try to get him out of the car and, most important, try to attract others to your car.

"What if someone tries to snatch my purse?"

Purse snatchers often make their grabs on the run. If you hold on tightly, he probably won't be able to get it from you as he's moving forward. If he stops and tugs at your pocketbook, however, you want to be careful that he doesn't push you to the ground, a way that many women are injured by purse snatchers. Says Sergeant Barbara Guarino, "Resist the purse snatcher, but if he persists, give in."

The purse snatcher doesn't care about you, he wants the money, credit cards, perhaps keys and other valuables in your purse. He will hurt you if he has to, but he'd rather not. Hurting you might take time and he'd rather take the purse and run. Never carry anything in your pocketbook that is life or death to you. It may mean the latter:

> Mary Carson went to a Houston hospital to visit a friend. As she walked to her car in the hospital parking lot after the visit, a man grabbed her purse. Mrs. Carson, a strong woman of forty-three, yanked it back.
>
> The man told her he had to have that purse but Mrs. Carson said, "No. I have all my personal belongings in it and I need it. If you want my purse, you're going to have to kill me."
>
> The man then pulled out a gun and shot Mrs. Carson three times in the head. Then he ran away with the purse.
>
> Before she died, Mrs. Carson related the details to the police. The purse contained $5.00.

"What if I think someone is going to snatch my purse?"

Head for the nearest well-lighted restaurant, other business, or home. Otherwise, stash your pocketbook in the nearest mailbox. You can retrieve it later from the post office. And if you need to run but you're wearing high-heeled shoes, take them off. The spike of the shoe can be used as a weapon.

"What if I'm attacked in the street by an unarmed man?"

Don't panic. Keep your wits about you and use any of the following suggestions of the Chicago Police Department:

> Scream as loud as you can, then strike back fast. Aim for his vital spots and make it hurt!
>
> Gouge eyes with thumbs, scratch him with your fingernails.
>
> Bash temple, nose, or Adam's apple with your purse, holding it as if it were a book. Or use a book.
>
> Poke an umbrella into his midriff.
>
> Jab a knee into his groin.
>
> If you are attacked from behind, dig your heels into his instep . . . kick his shins. Batter his face with the back of your head. Grab his little finger and bend it back sharply.

The Chicago Police Department also notes that if you are frequently out after dark you should get formal instruction in self-defense. Judo, karate, and other self-defense techniques are taught at many YMCA-YWCA facilities, in the adult education programs of some colleges and universities, and by local judo and karate schools. Television and books can't give you the proper preparation since your response to a street attack must be instantaneous. That response will come only after long and personal training.

"What if I'm attacked by an unarmed man and I have a gun?"

The laws in your state almost certainly make it illegal for you to carry a concealed gun, knife, tear-gas projectile, or other weapon. A policewoman I talked with in New York did have a gun in her purse one day when she was off duty:

> I was walking on a residential street when three girls in their late teens attacked me from behind. They hit me over the head with a long stick. I was stunned. They were after my bag, but I held on.
>
> They hit me again and this time they drew blood, but I held onto the bag. We fought, the three of them against me. Then the bag broke and everything went all over the place. Including my gun. I lunged for it and so did one of them. She got it.
>
> She stuck the loaded gun in my stomach and swore at me while another one of them hit me over the head again.
>
> Then they took my money and my gun. I ended up with a concussion.

The policewoman was lucky she wasn't killed. A lethal weapon like a gun is often taken away from the victim and used against him or her. You can carry an umbrella or a walking stick and use that for self-protection. Or you can do some damage with everyday objects like a nail file or fingernail scissors, a pen or pencil, a rat-tail comb, a letter opener, a knitting needle, or hair spray (which will temporarily blind him). A pocket alarm that emits a loud noise when you activate it can also be used.

Whatever you carry, it must always be in your hands and ready for possible use. A letter opener will do you no good if it's sitting on the bottom of your pocketbook while a man is grabbing you.

Both New York and Los Angeles police departments recommend two things: carry keys in your hands at all times; have a metal police whistle attached to your key chain. The next best sound, after screaming, is blowing a police whistle. Blow it three times and you'll probably scare the attacker away. But if you have no time to blow a whistle, strike out with your keys. Practice holding one or two keys between your fingers right near the knuckles. This way you can either scratch or poke your assailant.

"What if I'm sure this unarmed man is going to kill me?"

If there's no way out, fight hard and fight dirty. Says Sergeant Lee Kirkwood, "Scream and kick, but don't just kick at him, kick through him. Be vicious!" Policewoman Joyce Holmes comments, "Most men think you're going to go for the groin. He'll protect himself there so go for his *eyes*. Use your keys or your fingernails and try to blind him. Then run."

Some women don't think they could ever fight dirty or scratch a man's eyes out. Most policewomen disagree. Says one, "I think your own animal instincts are going to make you fight and fight any way you can."

Mrs. Cynthia B. is a housewife who often walks her small dog at night. She is the wife of a policeman:

> It was dusk and I was wearing an old coat as I walked my cocker spaniel. I don't know where the man came from but he was tall and had a fake gun. I could tell it was plastic because I've seen a lot of real guns. "I want your money," he said.
> "I have none," I answered.
> "Where's your home?" he demanded. We were several doors from my house and I figured he didn't know which was mine.
> "No," I said. He got angry and bashed my head up against a stone wall. As I slumped to the ground, my hand went into my coat pocket. He reached down to hit me again. I pulled out my keys and poked and slashed at his face and eyes. He staggered off holding his face in his hands. I was just a little shaken up, but he fell bleeding on the grass. The police took him to the hospital.

"What if I'm attacked by a man with a gun or knife?"

Whatever he wants, agree to it, at first. According to the Metropolitan Police Department of Washington, D.C., obeying his commands "is not only important for your safety, but it often gives the criminal a false sense of security."

Depending upon his demands, the circumstances, and your values, you may want to submit. If he's got you in a dark alley and no one else is around and he has a knife at your throat, you have to submit. Or do you?

You can't scream in this situation but you can talk. Sergeant Genevieve Hauck of Los Angeles suggests, "Play along with him. Pretend to cooperate. Maybe say, "Let's go to my place. It's just around the corner." You don't want him to stab you and you don't want to get into his car. So you might try to convince him you want him and you can both go to your place, which is within walking distance.

"Don't plead with him," warns Sergeant Kirkwood. "His determination will be boosted by your apparent helplessness." Instead, play along, get out into the light, near other people and possible escape.

Holly was a college student in Detroit when the following incident happened. Her way may not be for everyone, but it sure worked for her:

> I was lost in thought about some damn exam as I walked home toward my apartment. It was night but I wasn't worried. Suddenly, this guy's arm grabs me and pulls me into an alley.
>
> At first I didn't know what the hell was going on but I found out quick. He put a knife against my head and said, "I'm going to f—— you."
>
> My mind was racing like mad as he backed me against a wall and started ripping my clothes off. He kept the knife at my head but I started talking like mad. Quietly though, because I didn't want him using that damn knife. I was talking and talking, and before I knew it I was telling him how good-looking he was, how strong, how I bet he was pretty good in bed.
>
> It did something to him. He stopped ripping my clothes off and he looked at me. I kept talking a mile a minute, all the time giving him some masculine prowess bull. Then I told him he really turned me on. I told him he really excited me and, right then and there, I'd give him a blow job.

That blew his mind. He probably had these sick fantasies about women wanting him and all that crap. So he pulled his pants down.

Now I was in control. While he stood there so proudly, I bent down and bit him so hard he ran off screaming!

I was feeling a little sick but I didn't run home. I walked.

You can tell him how manly he is, you can "turn on the sympathy" as Sergeant Guarino calls it, you can even tell some rapists unbelievable things and they'll believe them. This is what Carol, wife and mother of three, did:

I got a ride with a friend to a restaurant where I applied for a job. I'm a waitress and was out of work at the time. After I talked with the manager, I called my husband to pick me up. My car was in the shop but my husband wasn't home so I had something to eat.

A man was talking with the manager when I tried my husband again and he still wasn't home. The manager asked what the problem was and I told him. This other man offered me a ride. He seemed nice enough and he was talking with the manager but I didn't want him to bother.

I had some coffee, and this man, he said his name was Fred, joined me. He talked about his wife and kids, showed me pictures of them and was real friendly. I tried my husband again and he still wasn't home. So I accepted a ride with Fred.

Driving along, I was doing all the talking. I think it even took me a few moments to realize he wasn't driving the right way. I don't know how but we were suddenly near some woods and he had a knife. And he was talking crazy!

He started hitting me with the wooden end, bruising me, then he started cutting me. For no reason. And talking, but I don't know what he said. It didn't make sense. I started screaming and kicking and hitting, but I'm pretty small [five-foot-four]. It didn't do any good. He raped me.

Then the nightmare really started. Fred had a wife and kids all right. The thing is, he'd been in a mental institution twice and knew he'd go back if anyone found out what he'd just done. So he had to kill me!

I couldn't fight him or escape because he was stronger than me so I started telling him I had a husband and kids and I knew how important a family was. I was agreeing with him how much a family means. Then I told him he was a nice guy. I told him he was such a nice guy I wanted to see more of him.

He was so crazy he believed me. I said I'd like to date him and go out with him and do things. It didn't make any sense but I talked and talked. I told him he was good and kind and gentle. Me, with bruises all over and cuts and all from him. And he believed me.

I told him I could walk home and I'd call him and we'd go out. He didn't want me to walk home, he wanted to drive me. I was afraid to let him see where I live because I have a teen-age daughter. But I had to take a chance.

He drove me home and walked me to the door. As soon as the door opened, I lunged inside and told my husband not to go out. We called the police and told them Fred's license number. My boy saw it. The police got Fred.

One comment on this true story: Carol wasn't drinking coffee in the restaurant. She and Fred had a few cocktails. That's why she doesn't remember some details.

"What if I'm attacked by an armed man who is drunk or high on drugs and talk will do no good?"

Alcohol is involved in a great many rapes. (When a woman has also been drinking, she has much less chance of escaping, since she can't react as well.) I talked with one convicted rapist who had been taking some pills with two buddies when they decided to rape the girl friend of one of the guys. There was absolutely nothing that woman could do when attacked by three men out of their heads with drugs.

When attacked by one drunk or drugged man, armed or unarmed, you can pretend to faint. If you can summon the presence of mind to attempt this, then he may put his weapon aside to sexually assault you, or he may use two hands to get you toward his car. In either case, you may have some chance of escape by faking a faint.

I talked with a man who raped a woman when he was drunk. He met her in a bar where she was a waitress and he got the definite feeling that she was interested in him. After more drinks, he was sure he was irresistible so he waited for her. After work, he tried to force himself on her but she rebuffed him. They fought, he won.

This man, call him R.B., used no knife or gun. He is short and slight of build, was pretty drunk at the time, yet he subdued a fairly young woman. How could he do that?

> Sometimes when I get drinking, I get strong, you know? Real strong. I've always had this very strong sex drive so I guess the two of them together made me do wrong. I know I did wrong.
>
> But, you know, sometimes women lead you on, sometimes they want things too. You know? And this woman, she was drinking too. Else she could have run away.
>
> [Can you suggest ways women can prevent this situation?] Of course. Don't drink. A drunk guy can't run after a sober woman, right?

"What if there's no escape. Must I just lie there?"

No. One New York detective says, "If you're being sexually assaulted, note any distinguishing characteristics of the guy. I had a rape case where the woman noted a shoulder scar. That's what was the predominant identifying feature. Also remember any property he takes or any surface areas he touches. This is the only defense during actual rape."

I can't let this chapter end on such a note so I'm including one last case history. It comes from Burbank, California:

> He was a short, thin man, so high on booze that he staggered into an alley. There he waited with longing for a female . . . any female. Soon, his hopes were answered. A very large, very drunk woman lumbered along nearby.
>
> He attacked her with delight.
>
> The police were called shortly thereafter as neighbors reacted to screams. It seems that the large woman ended up sitting on top of the scrawny man and enjoying their pleasure so much she wouldn't get off. He was the one yelling for the cops.

Incidentally, no one was booked in this case. The woman had no complaint against the man and the man only wanted to get away fast.

11

Hitchhiking

"I won't hurt anyone and no one will hurt me."

Those are the words of an eighteen-year-old, Maureen Hattem, a lively, affectionate young woman with wonderful dreams of the future. Her parents, Maurice and Iris Hattem, talk of Maureen with strength and love and tears in their eyes.

A few months after she turned eighteen, Maureen moved out of her comfortable suburban home to be on her own with some friends. She and her parents saw each other most weekends, met her new friends, and shared many experiences.

Last November 21 was a day of talk and laughter together. Then Maurice and Iris said good-by to their daughter. "She put her little cheek up for us to kiss," says Iris. "It was the last time we saw her."

Later that afternoon, Maureen and her boy friend hitchhiked toward March Air Force Base in Riverside, California. The first two rides were uneventful.

Then a young man in a four-wheel-drive vehicle picked them up. He was quiet but likable and interested in this couple. He never took them to the Air Force base. Instead, he made a "wrong turn" and drove off into a secluded area.

Maureen and her boy friend got nervous but the young driver just told them he'd go up a little farther, then turn around. He didn't. He stopped, threw the boy friend out of the car, took out a gun, and shot at him. The boy friend was dazed by the bullet.

Then the driver drove off with Maureen.

Two weeks later they found her. Maureen had been raped and murdered. Her killer has never been found.

Hitchhiking should be a great way to get around. You can meet people, learn things, and see places, all for free. You just stick out your thumb and off you go. Hitchhiking should be a convenient, groovy, fun way to travel. The problem is, it isn't.

Every day, hitchhikers are robbed, raped, physically assaulted, forced to commit unnatural acts, and murdered. Every day in Los Angeles alone there are three violent crimes related to hitchhiking that are reported to police. Some of these crimes, including both homosexual and heterosexual assaults, are committed by drivers, while hitchhikers commit the others. No one knows how many crimes related to hitchhiking in Los Angeles go unreported. No one knows how many hitchhiking crimes occur across the country.

Most hitchhikers and most drivers who pick them up do not plan to commit a crime. Some do. Some others act on impulse. Because of these people, hitchhiking is too dangerous for all hitchhikers and for all drivers. Police all over the country say, "Do not hitch-hike. Do not pick up hitchhikers."

For some people, however, hitchhiking is more an attitude than an action. It is part of a life-style, an element in a way of life that says you should do things free and easy, that everyone should love one another, that "I won't hurt anyone and no one will hurt me." Other people hitchhike knowing that something bad can happen but confident that they can handle it. And there are a few people who are afraid to hitchhike but do it anyway because they feel there is no other way to get where they're going.

The following information is all factual. It primarily concerns women drivers and women hitchhikers because they run the bigger risks. The purpose of this chapter is to get you to stop picking up hitchhikers and to stop you from hitchhiking. But if nothing is going to change your mind and you're going to continue picking up hitchhikers or you're going to continue to hitchhike, then I'll give you some tips that might help you prevent hitchhiking crimes.

If you don't want to be safe, maybe I can help you be a little safer.

DRIVERS

Most women who pick up hitchhikers pick up only girls so that the girls won't be picked up by guys. "A woman who picks up a man or a man and a girl is asking for it," says Officer Ken Harris of Los Angeles. "In fact, anyone who picks up any hitchhiker, man or woman, is opening the door to trouble." Officer Harris, a handsome crime-prevention policeman in his late twenties, has several years experience with felonies related to hitchhiking:

> The typical scam I used to cover was a guy and girl hitchhiking along a main street in Los Angeles or Hollywood. Some man or woman would pick up the couple. Either the guy or the girl would get in back, it didn't matter which, and while the other would be talking to the driver, the one in back would pull out a knife and put it to the driver's neck.
>
> The couple would then force the driver to drive to some secluded spot, usually in the Hollywood hills. Then they'd rob the driver of everything he or she had, kick him out of the car, and drive off.
>
> By the time the driver got to a phone to call us, the couple would be many miles away.

There are variations on this crime, including the most direct hit: a girl stands alone, a car stops, her boy friend jumps out of some nearby trees with a gun or a knife. The couple robs the driver or they rob him *and* steal his car. "The car can stop, the guy jump out, rob the driver, and get away with his car all in about thirty seconds." It happens that fast.

A girl alone can pull this scam. More often, girl hitchhikers will do

other things, such as enticing a guy back to an apartment where a
male confederate is waiting to rob him.

Although these robberies and thefts occur every day, even more
common is a crime that is seldom reported. An innocent-looking
girl hitchhikes alone, pulls her theft without a gun or knife, and
almost always gets away. One girl who claimed she never did this
told me how it's done:

> You look for straight guys. A clean car, maybe a family car
> like a guy in a station wagon. You're looking for a family man.
> That's the thing. You hitchhike only during the day and on
> busy streets where there's lots of traffic.
>
> Dress the part, too. You wear something real innocent,
> carrying books and all. Or you can look sexy with hot pants
> and no bra. Depends on how you feel.
>
> Anyway, you put out your thumb when the right guy comes
> along. Hop in and talk and all. Then, when you're stopped at
> a traffic light and lots of cars are all around, you tell him, "Give
> me twenty dollars or I'll yell 'Rape.'"
>
> He'll stammer something or other and he won't believe you
> so you tell him, "I mean it. Twenty dollars or I yell 'Rape.'"
>
> Man, they fork over that money fast!

Lieutenants Frank Isbell and Glen Sherman of the Los Angeles
Police Department are conducting surveys on hitchhikers and those
who pick them up. According to these two authorities, some innocent-looking girls do more than threaten to yell rape. "We've
heard of girls," says Lieutenant Isbell, "who rip open their blouse
and say, 'Give me everything you've got.' If the guy hesitates,
she'll tell him she's under eighteen and he'll be busted for statutory
rape."

Without trying to, the hitchhiker can cause a driver problems.
How? Drugs. If the hitchhiker has some drugs on him or her and the
police pull the car over and find these drugs, both the hitchhiker and
the driver will be booked on narcotics charges. Similarly, if there's
an accident and drugs are found in the car, both the hitchhiker and
the driver are booked.

Then there's another thing that hitchhikers often bring into cars:
the elements. If it's raining, they make things wet; if it's windy or

snowing, they bring in the cold; and if it's hot, they bring in body odor.

This is unfair to the hitchhikers who simply want to travel without hassling anyone, who break no laws, plan no rip-offs, are clean of drugs and dirt and are dry, warm, and sweet-smelling. But no matter how many truly innocent hitchhikers there are, the others who will hurt you, intentionally or unintentionally, should cause you to pass by all hitchhikers. You may not be fair to the many but you will be safe from the few. In the words of Lieutenant Isbell, "I wouldn't advise anybody to pick up any hitchhiker, I don't care who it is."

DRIVER PRECAUTIONS

You may still want to pick up hitchhikers occasionally. Perhaps you think, "I can size up a hitchhiker in a second and drive on if I don't like what I see." Lots of people claim this ability, and if you're one of them, no one can tell you it's impossible. So here are some precautions a driver can take before he or she picks up hitchhikers:

> Before you stop, see if anyone may be hiding nearby. Perhaps there are more hitchhikers than you want to pick up. Perhaps someone is planning to jump out and rob you.
>
> And realize, before you stop, that you are about to let one or more strangers very close to you while most of your attention will be focused on handling a potentially deadly weapon, your car.
>
> Before you let them in, get to know as much as possible about the hitchhikers. Make them talk. Listen not only to their words but their ability or inability to speak coherently. Are they nervous or fidgety? Have they been drinking? And look them in the eye when you talk. Will they look you in the eye or is something wrong? Do their eyes look "funny"? Are the eyes red, dilated, glassy, tearing. In other words, can you tell if they are on some drug?
>
> If you let just one in you're a little safer than if you let in two or more. If one of them gets in back, keep your eyes on the road and on all of them.

A hidden tape recorder can record all events but it can't prevent any trouble. If you tell them there's a tape recorder, they'll ruin it.

If there's trouble, talk. You can talk your way out of some crimes. Turn on the sympathy, pretend to compromise, stall, do whatever you can until you can drive some place for help.

And remember that you're still in the driver's seat. You're the one handling that deadly weapon, your car. As a last resort, when you're sure they'll kill you with the knife against your neck, threaten to kill them too unless they throw their weapons out the window.

But it's usually not that dramatic. They will, instead, deny that any harm will come to you. They "just want some money." When the car is stopped and they are in complete control, they have you.

All of this assumes that hitchhiking is legal. It's illegal in Colorado and Washington, on most interstate highways, in New York City and other cities, and the list is growing. Check on this in your area or you may have trouble even before the hitchhikers get into your car.

HITCHHIKERS

When a girl puts out her thumb, most men immediately think, "She's asking for it." And the "it" is sex. These men reason: if a girl will step into my car without knowing me, she'll go to my home, too.

Actually, getting into a strange man's car is more dangerous than going to his home. He can drive you to a deserted place where screams will bring no help. And even if he intends no harm, he might be a bad driver. When you get into a car with a complete stranger, you are putting your life in his hands.

The girl hitchhikers I have talked with know they're taking some chances. "I figure he doesn't want to get killed so he'll drive okay," says one. And the girl hitchhikers also know that men have sex on their minds. In fact some of the girls look as sexually provocative as possible so they'll be sure of a ride. "Oh, they hint about sex lots of times and sometimes I get a proposition," says one girl, "but it's nothing I can't handle."

Some of these girls are pretty choosey about the rides they accept. One young woman who has hitchhiked across the country maintains, "I can tell the guy's vibrations. If they're good, I get in. If not, I say, 'No, thanks,' and wait for another ride."

Then there are girls who have "no hang-ups" about sex. According to one girl, "A friend of mine will stop off in the bushes with a guy. I mean, she wants a ride and will give him what he wants." Another girl told of a girl friend who "was raped but hasn't told her parents because they'd be upset she was hitchhiking."

Most parents are upset when they know their daughters (and sons) are hitchhiking. The thing is, most parents don't know. According to the surveys of female teen-age hitchhikers that Lieutenants Isbell and Sherman have been conducting, "Over 90 per cent of the parents don't know that their daughters are hitchhiking. Almost all of these parents strongly disapprove of the practice."

These lieutenants also have numerous case histories of male drivers who pick up female (or male) hitchhikers and force oral copulation; male drivers who pick up female hitchhikers and masturbate in front of them; male drivers who pick up female (or male) hitchhikers and fondle and assault them . . . all of this while the car is in motion.

And when the car is brought to a stop, there are "far too many cases of rapes and murders," says Lieutenant Isbell.

The following letter is self-explanatory. The name of the young woman who wrote it has been withheld:

Dear Los Angeles Police:

Though it is an unpleasant incident that I would rather forget, I am writing to you in hopes that some other girl can be protected from similar harassment.

When I was hitchhiking in downtown Monterey, I was picked up by a medium-sized man with blondish brown hair and blue eyes. To make a long story short, the classic terror occurred, he drove me off on a side road and threatened to rape me with a knife held close to me. He told me he has been in and out of [mental hospitals] and had run-ins with the police because he has raped other girls. Yet, when they pressed charges, there was nothing the police could do because they didn't have enough evidence. . . .

I talked to him and either he lost his nerve or else he meant it as a sick joke, because after enjoying my fear he finally drove me back onto 101. I have great pity for someone with such problems, but obviously it would be better if his deviance took a more harmless form.

I contacted the Berkeley police on my return and they told me to write to any police department he would be near. He told me he travels up and down between San Francisco and Los Angeles. I hope that you will stop every girl you see hitch-hiking by herself and ask her if she loves life, and tell her that when somebody holds a knife up to her throat and threatens to take her life away, she's going to think of all the dawns and laughs and oceans she's going to miss, and she's going to wish she took the bus and paid the quarter, instead of taking a risk. If you trust people, it's hard to believe it can happen, but unfortunately some people were so scarred by home situations, etc. that they do vent it back on society in general. Tell any girls you see not to wait for it to happen, not to come that close. Tell them it's not parents and police and all the authority figures that say it, it's another girl who learned by a really close brush. I don't want it to happen to anyone else.

Thank you.

Even this moving plea is discounted by some confirmed hitch-hikers who claim that this girl would have been safe if she'd hitch-hiked with a guy or even another girl. Maureen Hattem hitchhiked with her boy friend. What happened to him is what usually happens to the passengers the driver doesn't want to keep. One police expert explains, "The driver will stop and let out one or two hitchhikers, but he'll hold onto the one he wants and start off before she can exit. Or he'll take a gun or a knife and force the others out. Then the remaining girl is faced with a man holding a deadly weapon. That situation she can't handle."

Says a pretty coed, "But when you miss the bus and another doesn't come along for about an hour, you've got to get to class any way you can. Besides, I only takes rides with other students."

In some areas of the country, public transportation is grossly inadequate. The lack of mass transit definitely influences some girls to hitchhike. Other girls, however, in the same situation, don't hitchhike. The girl who must get to class on time will sooner or later not be careful when she's running late. And there is no way around the fact that hitchhiking is dangerous.

If lack of public transportation or wanting to do what is "in" or something else causes you to hitchhike, talk it over with your parents. They will be concerned that you feel you need to hitchhike and may be able to help you find alternate transportation. The answer may be a bicycle, a scooter, a motorcycle, or a car of your own. The answer may be a car pool, prearranged rides with friends, or introductions to friends of friends. The answer may also be pressure on local, state, and federal governments to improve mass-transit systems. Talk with your folks.

HITCHHIKING PRECAUTIONS

Sometimes parents won't listen. Sometimes young people won't talk. Whatever the reasons, some people are going to hitchhike. They may even treat the dangers with a sign, as did two girls I saw recently. The words on their sign: "No perverts please!"

The precautions that follow don't include how to tell a pervert from a healthy man. Rely on your instincts, follow the tips below, and maybe you'll be all right. Although the girls holding the sign didn't know it, they also carried another sign at their feet: two sleeping bags. Lieutenant Sherman has observed, "If a man intends to rape or kill a hitchhiker, he may look for one with a sleeping bag. The sleeping bag shows that this hitchhiker is out on her own and won't be missed for quite a while."

> Girls should never hitchhike alone. Hitchhike with a guy (though he may want some favors) if possible or with other girls.
> Before getting in, talk with the driver. Make him talk to you. Don't just tell him where you're going, find out where he's going. If possible, go around to the driver's side to get closer

to him. Look him in the eye, see if he looks sick or drunk or drugged. Smell him, too. Don't be afraid to say, "No, thanks."

Never accept a ride with someone who has passed you, circled the block, and come back for you. This man is thinking about more than where he's going.

Avoid hitchhiking early in the morning and after dark, when more people are out looking for girls and there are less cars that might offer help.

Don't accept rides with more than one guy in the car, no matter how many are in your party.

Don't take a ride that will leave you stranded. Accept only rides that will let you off in populated areas after traveling along main routes.

If some driver hassles you, move away from the road. If there's no place to go, walk down the road in the opposite direction of traffic. The driver will have to turn around or risk backing up against traffic.

Always sit next to the door. Never sit between two men, never sit right next to the driver, and never sit in the back seat of a two-door car.

You might want to carry a legal "weapon" with you. The weapon should look innocent but provide some means of defense. I know of one guy who always carries a boomerang. More popular is a full soft-drink bottle that can both quench your thirst and be used as a club.

Before the car takes off, check your door. Be sure you can open it. Some cars have automatic door-lock devices controlled by the driver. A rapist in L.A. and another in Maine have removed the passenger's door handles.

Expect to be propositioned, especially if you're hitchhiking alone or with a girl friend. If you're a girl with a girl friend, you might want to indicate that you're lesbians. That'll turn some guys off.

Sometimes a perfectly "healthy" driver will begin to think that this strange girl or girls or couple offers him some golden opportunity for a crime he'll probably get away with. He didn't plan anything. The opportunity just came right to him.

Other precautions:

Watch out if the driver starts behaving nervously, stops talking and seems involved with unspoken thoughts, changes speed drastically (either slows way down or speeds way up), or takes a wrong turn.

You're a little safer to take rides only within a city or suburb on surface streets. There's bound to be some traffic lights or stop signs that will make the driver stop and enable you to jump out unhurt.

Never jump out of a moving car. He can force oral copulation, he can fondle you, and he can masturbate, but he almost surely won't kill you when the car is moving fast. And you almost surely will kill yourself if you jump out of a car at high speed.

If you're traveling along and he pulls out a gun or a knife, try not to panic. Instead, look around for some car behind you. Say something like, "Hey, those are my friends, the ones I was going to meet. There they are right behind us." And wave. Then tell him he'd better drop you off at the side of the road or the next exit but very soon! If you're lucky, it'll work.

If not, panic will only ensure harm. Stay calm. Try to talk him out of whatever he's got in mind. As you've seen from the letter included above, steady, reasoned talk can help.

The majority of hitchhiking rides go off without much trouble. Sometimes there's some bad talk, but the action usually doesn't match it. When an uneventful ride is about to end, don't let your guard down:

> The girl or girls should always get out of the car first. And they should move away from the car, out of arm's reach. Hold hands with your fellow hitchhikers as you get out to try to make sure that everyone does get out.

And, a last point, make sure where and how you're hitchhiking isn't against the law. Most often you can't stand on the road nor can you sit on the shoulder. You must stand on the shoulder. There's no hitchhiking on many major highways and freeways, though sometimes you can thumb a ride on the approaches.

Because there are so many crimes related to hitchhiking, the number of towns and cities and counties and states that make it illegal is growing. You'll get some pretty heavy fines if you don't keep abreast of the latest information on these laws.

Maurice and Iris Hattem spend a great deal of time campaigning for laws against hitchhiking and for other laws to help protect young people. Their work helps assuage the loss of their daughter, Maureen. Mrs. Hattem has also kept a notebook of her thoughts to help her cope with her new situation, and has consented to share portions of this notebook.

There was a two-week period when Maureen was missing and believed kidnaped:

> I had believed up to the last that we would find her alive and well. I had prayed *believing* this, and my faith was really shaken! I had always considered myself a Christian, but I had much to learn about being a Christian!
>
> There is no guarantee that trials and tribulations, problems and sorrows will not come to you, just because you're a Christian. . . .
>
> I put a small picture of Maureen on the ledge near the sink in the kitchen that I could see as I went about my daily work. Her eyes seemed to talk to me and I could almost hear her say, "I'm all right, Mom." Each morning I would look at her picture and repeat the 121st Psalm, "I will lift up my eyes unto the hills, from whence cometh my help. My help cometh from the Lord which maketh Heaven and Earth." I found this a great help, even though it seemed that I was almost hypnotizing myself.
>
> What a wonderful legacy she left us! From her birth, which I was awake to witness, she brought joy into the world. . . . Those years as we watched her grow she was sweet, shy, ambitious, and independent. After she had overcome the period of "braces on her teeth," she seemed more confident, less shy. She became creative and practical in her school work, but never boastful. . . .
>
> She was truly feminine! Wouldn't use a deodorant if it didn't smell just so and she collected colognes and perfumes—liked the shapes of bottles and especially their contents—they just had to suit her tastes!
>
> We used to laugh at all her "beauty tips"! Especially her

dried milk and oatmeal baths—called her Cleopatra. Her eyes were her best feature. They were blue-green, depending on what she wore, her mood, or the type of day. She knew how to use eye make-up—had a special knack—not too much, not too little. Otherwise she didn't use make-up—she didn't have to. . . .

Sometimes my loneliness for her overwhelms me, and I am unable to continue whatever I am doing—I must withdraw, let my emotions go—and cry buckets of tears! I try to keep myself occupied, but nothing interests me for long. I can almost become enthusiastic at times, but not for long. I come down with a thump when reality catches up with me, and I realize for the thousandth time that Maureen is dead!

12

After a Theft, Mugging, or Rape

I was working on a biology paper when I realized a friend down the hall had a book of mine that I needed. So I ran down and got it. I returned and resumed studying but, after a while, something caught my eye and I looked up. Standing right near me was a big, ugly man.

There wasn't time to scream or kick or fight. It was over very fast.

But I was damned if he was going to get away unpunished. Not after what he'd just done to me. So I told him I liked him, I told him I liked being taken so forcefully by such a strong man. We made a date for the following evening at my place.

He was back the next night and I was waiting for him. So were the police.

The speaker in this case history is a college student in New York City. Over half (57 per cent) of all reported rapes are solved and about half (49 per cent) of all suspected rapists brought to trial have their cases dismissed and/or acquitted. The number of rapes that go unsolved, plus the number of perpetrators who go unpunished, plus the number of rapes that go unreported totals a great many rapists in our society. This coed was taking no chances on her assailant getting away!

When any crime is over, it really isn't over. It is time for good people to make sure that the guilty parties get punished. Unfortunately, that's a lot easier said than done.

LARCENY AND AUTO THEFT

Only 20 per cent of all larceny offenses (such as pick pocketing) brought to police attention are solved. That means your chances of getting any of your stolen goods back or of justice being done are, at best, one in five.

What can you do to help after the crime is committed? Not too much. But among the ways you can help get some justice are by observing as much as possible about the perpetrator; knowing what was in your wallet or pocketbook, including the account numbers of your credit cards; and calling the police immediately.

Most often, the purse snatcher will run with the purse and keep running as he sorts through it, discarding the bag itself and any other items he doesn't want. It is possible that the police can find these nonmonetary items for you. And it is highly probable that your call to the police will bring about an increase in foot or car patrols of the area. Perhaps even plainclothesmen and women pretending to be shoppers will walk where you walked in hopes of catching the purse snatcher.

Larceny involving items stolen from cars is committed in such a tremendous number of instances that the police have a tough time solving these cases. An additional problem are the investigations launched after a citizen reports a theft, then the citizen finds that the goods were misplaced or lent to a friend and were not stolen. Before notifying the police, be sure you are actually missing the items and be as positive as possible that they were stolen.

Time is of the essence after any crime. You want to report to the police immediately, but you also want to be sure a crime has actually occurred. In some cases, you'll have to use your best judgment as to when you have secured enough proof that you did, for example, leave your coat in your car and someone did enter your car and take it. Other times, of course, it will be obvious that a crime has occurred.

Many people report stolen cars that, in fact, haven't been stolen. The people have merely forgotten where they parked them. If your car is stolen, contact the police immediately. If you should be near your car when it's being stolen, *never* try to stop the thieves. That's too dangerous. Instead, get a description of them.

Over two thirds (69 per cent) of all stolen cars are returned to their owners, though many of these cars are damaged or stripped of accessories. Only 17 per cent of all auto thefts, however, result in the arrest of the offender. You can help by knowing your license number and your vehicle identification number (VIN). Take a moment, find these numbers (the VIN is located on the dashboard near the windshield in front of the steering wheel and on your car registration). Then write down these numbers on a piece of paper that you always carry in your wallet. That way you'll have these numbers when you need them.

Also be familiar with the make and model, year and color of your car plus any distinguishing features. If you or your man has a business card, the Dallas police suggest that you slide it alongside a window so that it falls inside the panel door. Or put your name on a blank file card and do the same. You can also scratch your initials inside the trunk or under the hood. After your car is stolen you will also want to contact your insurance agent.

MUGGING

All muggings are a form of robbery. Some offenders threaten to use force but don't, others injure their victims. If the perpetrator should take little or even nothing, be sure to contact the police so they can pinpoint crimes in your area and better combat them.

If you are injured, yell for help as soon as the offender has left. If you can move, go to any door—business or residential, lighted or dark—and ask the people inside to call the police. They may be too scared to help, but they will call the police for you.

By contacting the police, you can get help for yourself, you can help protect your neighbors from similar attacks, and you can also apply for government compensation. California, New York, Nevada,

Hawaii, Massachusetts, Maryland, and New Jersey award money to innocent victims of crime. The maximum amount that can be paid ranges from a low of $5,000 in California (though through state legislation, that may rise to $25,000) to a high of $45,000 in Maryland.

The federal government is considering similar legislation that is more generous. Perhaps by the time you read this, innocent victims of crime can be compensated up to $50,000 for medical injuries and loss of income. The proposed federal program is even more generous to the passer-by who is injured while coming to the aid of a victim.

Few people take advantage of the existing compensation programs, however, because most people don't know about them. If you or a loved one or a friend is a victim of a crime, be sure to check with your state government (whether it's mentioned above or not) to see if you can be awarded either state or federal funds.

RAPE

If you are confronted by any criminal, you will want to be able to describe him to the police. See the illustration and other materials on describing suspects in Chapter 6. In some cases, women have been forcibly raped yet have not seen the man's face, nor have they been able to observe any distinguishing characteristics of his, nor have they seen how he fled.

After attacking Judy, a case history related in Chapter 10, the rapist went on to assault several other women and girls. One of his victims didn't get a good look at him, but after he left she thought she heard a Volkswagen drive away. Another of his victims could tell the police only that her assailant drove some sort of red car. From then on, the police were looking for a red Volkswagen, and they soon had their man.

After a rape, the victim should call for help when it's safe or, if possible, go the nearest residence or business and have them call the police. Any and all information given to the police will help apprehend the offender.

Most women who have been forcibly raped, however, do not report the crime to the police. While 46,430 rapes were brought to the attention of the police in 1972, I have heard experts estimate that from five times that number (about 230,000 forcible rapes) to twenty times that number (about 920,000 forcible rapes) actually occur every year.

Why don't women report this crime? There are many reasons. Among them are the various ways women react to being forcibly raped. Holly, the student who bit the would-be rapist, didn't report him because he was unsuccessful. I have heard of other women who haven't reported forcible rapes because the offender was black and these white women didn't think he'd get a fair trial.

Then there are women who are not physically injured nor are they very upset about the incident and don't want to bother reporting it. At the other extreme are the victims who react so adversely to the crime that they can't talk about it with anyone.

Dr. Robert Alan Cole, a psychiatrist who works with sex criminals, has some advice for victims of rape who are broken up by the assault:

> It is not the rape itself that is the determining factor but the reaction of the victim and the victim's relatives and friends to the rape. If everyone feels that rape is the worst thing in the world, it will be the worst thing in the world.
>
> But if everyone feels that the rape is very bad but not horrible, then the victim will not be too adversely affected.

Some women, particularly young and elderly women, find their lives so shattered after being forcibly raped that they are temporarily or permanently unable to function. It is for the sake of these women that the other women should report attempted or actual rapes. Sergeant Genevieve Hauck elaborates:

> A rapist is sick. Even if he has been drinking or taking pills that lower his inhibitions, he is sick. If he gets away with rape the first time, he will rape again. And again.
>
> The rapist needs help because he is sick. There will be other victims and he may severely injure a woman. Maybe his next victim will die of a heart attack.

Reporting a rape can sometimes, however, lead to problems. While *you* know the rape occurred, the police and the district attorney's office will want proof. A New York detective explains, "A gynecologist will examine the woman for semen and for tears.

Even an experienced woman might have tears of tissue if she has been forcibly raped. Ripped clothing, including torn panties plus any cuts or bruises, are evidence needed to prove rape."

In a state like New York, you must be able to prove that force was used, that the victim was afraid, that the victim attempted to resist, that the offender did penetrate, that the suspect is the offender, *and* all of these must be corroborated. Since witnesses are seldom around to corroborate a victim's claim of rape, many rapists go free.

Most other states have laws that do *not* require anywhere near the total corroboration of New York, and some, like California, have noncorroboration laws. Everywhere, however, rape is easy to charge and hard to prove. Much of the time the conviction depends not upon hard evidence but upon attitudes of the police, the judge, and the jurors toward the suspect and the victim. If, for example, the victim is very young or very old, the suspect is very closely scrutinized. But if the victim is in her late teens or early twenties, is pretty and has slept with more than one man in her life, juries often scrutinize her very closely.

My interviews with police and with rape victims indicate that the police, generally speaking, are skeptical of most rape reports. Although official national figures show 18 per cent of reported forcible rapes prove to be unfounded, unofficial estimates by several police officers indicate some four out of five reported forcible rapes were not truly forcible nor was the woman nonconsenting at the time. One policewoman told me, "What often happens is that a woman wants to make love to a man and does but is either discovered outright or gives her husband or regular boy friend a venereal disease. Then she yells, 'Rape.' Or a couple are petting heavily and have intercourse before she can stop him or they can stop themselves. A little later, because she's scared, the young woman will sometimes claim that she was raped."

A woman raped by a man she knows well will probably have some difficulty getting the police to believe her. Close friends might have some questions, too. On the other hand, a woman who is raped by a total stranger or by someone she scarcely knows will usually find the police completely cooperative.

If you are raped you must contact the police as soon after as possible. The claim filed one or more days after the crime is automatically suspect. It is also hard to prove because the life of the semen is only about eight to ten hours. After you have been checked by a gynecologist for semen and tears, you will want to have an antiseptic douche. (If you have a douche before a doctor examines you, then of course you destroy the semen that can be used as evidence.) You also want a shot of penicillin to guard against venereal disease.

The rape itself can be a shocking experience. What I'm trying to do here is let you know the truth: events after the rape can sometimes be rough. I also present the difficulties so you will take precautions that will prevent a rapist from attacking you or your loved ones.

By no means, however, is it always difficult after a rape. Judy, who was forced to commit oral copulation, had only one complaint about the police and the court system. "The first officer, the one who came right after I called the police, he was more interested in dating my roommate than in getting the information about me. A few weeks later, a detective talked to me and he was very nice. Then, in court, it wasn't difficult. The cross-examination was okay."

While Judy's assailant was the suspect in several rapes, R.B. was involved in only one act of rape. Yet the woman he attacked made sure to call the police, to undergo the tests they needed, to cooperate fully with them and with the district attorney and the courts. That's how she made sure R.B. was put in prison for several years and is still watched closely by his parole agent.

If you or a loved one or a friend is raped but the criminal act is not reported, then the rapist remains at loose to attack others. He may attack the same people again, or he may go after young girls, or elderly women.

Also, his sickness will keep feeding on him. As long as he has no help, he will remain sick. He needs help and, almost undoubtedly, will get it only under a court-prescribed system.

Although it is much better to report a rape immediately, if the act occurred some time in the recent past and wasn't reported, you might have some information the police can use to catch the criminal. Your case probably won't convict him because too much time has elapsed, but your description of him, his M.O., or his car may be instrumental in his capture.

After a rape, call the police. That's the best way to help yourself and other women.

13

Crimes Within the Family

Most murders are committed by relatives of the victim or persons acquainted with the victim. It follows, therefore, that criminal homicide is, to a major extent, a national social problem beyond police prevention. In 1971 [and 1972], killings within the family made up about one-fourth of all murders.

FBI Uniform Crime Reports—1971

Most aggravated assaults, rapes, and child molestings also occur within the family unit, among neighbors or acquaintances. These crimes usually take place in the home of either the offender or the victim and the emotions of one or both parties are so intense that the illegal acts are often called "crimes of passion."

As the above quotation states, there is little the police can do to prevent these crimes. One detective goes even further. He states, "Crimes within the family are crimes that no one can prevent."

There is little preventive action the police can take regarding these crimes. But some of the murders, aggravated assaults, rapes, and child molestings among people who know each other can be prevented. If you know some vital facts, sometimes you *can* prevent some of these crimes. Other times you *can* prevent a recurrence.

CHILD MOLESTING

Most people think that child molesters are scruffy-looking bums who wait around schoolyards with bags of candy and lure little children into the bushes or parked cars. It's not so. "Most child molesters are daddies and uncles and stepfathers," states Sergeant Barbara Guarino. A study conducted under a grant from the U. S. Children's Bureau of five hundred sex-crime and molestation victims showed that in 83 per cent of the cases, the offender belonged to the child's immediate environment. In 25 per cent of the cases, the offense was incestuous.

Some people think that child molesting occurs only among the lower classes. Sergeant Bud Carr of Los Angeles has investigated cases among all kinds of people. "Doctors, dentists, lawyers, workingmen, unemployed, *all* classes. I recently had a case where the offender, a father, lived in a $100,000 home and molested the neighbor kids after they swam in his pool."

I have pieced together the following case history from three counseling sessions that I attended with a parole agent, a husband and a wife. The husband, Lyle, is a Hollywood-handsome businessman in his late thirties who works in a clothing store. The wife, Cynthia, is in her mid-thirties, quite attractive, a housewife, and, lately, a secretary. Not present was seventeen-year-old June, a bright and beautiful college student. June is the natural daughter of Cynthia, the step-daughter of Lyle:

> Lyle has just been released from prison where he served four years for drug addiction (amphetamines) and child molesting (he molested June). Lyle, however, claims he never molested June, she enticed him. At the time, she was barely thirteen. Although Lyle will admit that his morals were very low four years ago, he maintains that Cynthia forced him.
>
> Cynthia was having an affair with another man. She says she was seeing this man because Lyle was seeing another woman. Lyle denies this and says that to get back at Cynthia, he didn't protest June's advances.
>
> June and Lyle's illicit relationship lasted three months. Lyle

says the length of the relationship is proof that June was not nearly as repulsed by it as she has always claimed.

All of that is in the past. But these two people still carry it in their heads and their hearts as they try to figure out where they are. June has now gone off to college. Lyle and Cynthia want to live together again, but they don't trust each other. They love each other, but they're afraid of each other. When they are together or apart, they remain very much alone and confused.

After three very long sessions, Lyle and Cynthia slowly began to realize that there is nothing left of their family. Among the many causes, amid the shared blame, the act that cannot be forgiven, that can never be accepted, is child molesting.

It is difficult for most of us to understand the thinking of a child molester. Taking advantage of a little boy or girl is the work of a person with a sick mind. One parole agent I met, however, had a slightly different view. When I asked him if he could introduce me to some child molesters, he said, "Sure. Some of my best friends are child molesters."

He was speaking ironically but truthfully. Some child molesters are very likable people. They are seemingly happy-go-lucky men, or jolly uncles, or friendly neighbors who love to play with kids. Unfortunately, their love for kids is not normal, though seldom does a child molester actually physically assault a child.

Sergeant Elizabeth Eggleston of Los Angeles has investigated many child molesting cases with her associates. "When we get deeply into a case," says Sergeant Eggleston, "we always find something abnormal between the husband and wife's sexual relationship." Sergeant Bud Carr, who often works with Sergeant Eggleston, continues: "Take one fairly typical case. The man and woman, both in their late twenties, were living together before they were married, but the guy wouldn't sleep with her. Now this man has a steady, professional job, always looks neat and clean and seems healthy to all who know him. But when his woman wants to know why he won't sleep with her, he answers, 'I'm saving myself until we're married.' Then they get married and he still won't sleep with her. The woman doesn't know what's going on but the man brings home a good paycheck and pays the bills so she doesn't say anything. Turns out the guy is a child molester."

Cindy, age seven, is one of the children who met up with this man:

> Her mother dropped off Cindy and some friends at a city swimming pool and planned to pick them all up. But some of the boys starting splashing water and flicking wet towels at Cindy so she decided she wanted to go home early. She changed and left the swimming pool in tears.
>
> Along the way home, a man stopped her and asked what she was crying about. She told him. "He looked like a nice man," Cindy would later tell the police. He offered to drive her home and she accepted, but then he stopped behind a supermarket. There, Cindy also told police. "He put his peepee in my mouth." When he was finished with her, the man dumped Cindy off in a vacant lot.

How can you prevent your children from being molested by strangers and by "friends"? Sergeant Eggleston advises, "Parents must be extremely vigilant. Beware when kids spend too much time playing with some man, be he a friend or neighbor or relative. Of course I'm not saying kids should never play with adults, but when you think they're playing too much of the time with certain adults, beware."

Sergeant Bud Carr adds, "Be alert if a child gets little presents from an adult, free ice cream from the ice-cream man, toys from a neighbor."

Since males compose the great majority of child molesters, Sergeant Carr has some advice concerning baby-sitters. "I would be very wary of having a male baby-sitter, teen-ager or college kid. Even the child next door. You may have known him for many years but you don't know his sex drives."

There are many cases of children molested in the home when their playmates are in another room and the wife is asleep in a bedroom. So Sergeant Carr also suggests, "Men shouldn't have little children in the house if their wife isn't up and around. I don't believe that a man should find himself in a position where he could be accused of child molesting."

Some strangers, however, will bother children. Child psychotherapist Patricia Powers of Los Angeles says, "You don't want to teach the child that all strangers are dangerous but that some may hurt boys and girls. In case the child doesn't know what a stranger is, you can define it as someone neither the child's mommy or daddy knows or, for an older child, someone the child has never met before."

Several police departments offer basic rules that will help prevent children being molested by strangers. The following list is supplied by the Detroit Police Department:

> Always go straight to school and directly home from school.
> Walk with other classmates whenever possible, following the sidewalks.
> Play where it is safe: backyards, playgrounds, etc. Never play in alleys or streets.
> Never play in vacant buildings or houses, or around construction areas.
> Never talk to or go with strangers even though they ask for directions, assistance in finding a lost dog, offer money, candy, or toys, or a ride in a car.
> Never let strangers in your home. Only grown-ups should open doors and let in properly identified people.
> Children who must utilize a public restroom should be accompanied by an adult.
> Try to remember or write down the license number of the car, or the description of any stranger who approaches you.
> Always notify your parents, teacher, or the police of any suspicious person or incident.
> NOTE TO PARENTS: An explanation and periodic review of these rules will contribute greatly to the safety of your child.

The Police Department of Des Moines suggests two additional points. "Advise children that police officers are their friends and will always help them. Do not use the police officer as a threat to make children behave." The second suggestion concerns Blue Star Homes in Des Moines, or Block Parents in some other areas. "Show your children the Blue Star Homes in your area—homes to go to if they need help or assistance." These special homes are the result of cooperation between PTAs and the police. A child who is lost, injured, or bothered by a potential child molester can receive immediate help from the adult in one of these approved homes. (Your PTA or police department should have information on Blue Star Homes or a Block Parent Program.)

The most effective means of preventing child molesting from strangers or people known to your child is communication. You want to talk with your child and make sure he or she understands what you're saying and will ask you questions or tell you events that have occurred. If your child asks what a child molester does, child psychotherapist Patricia Powers suggests, "You can tell the child this man might hurt you, be mean to you, pinch you, or cut you. Relate a child molester's possible actions not to sex but to some experience the child has had, such as getting fingers caught in a door."

The approach you use is very important not only because of the delicate nature of the subject but because of the much broader subject of sex. Authorities suggest de-emphasizing any threatening aspects and stressing positive, normal, healthy behavior such as, "Good strangers leave children alone." This quotation from the Seattle police is offered along with the following approach to teaching rules regarding child molesting:

> A calm, matter-of-fact, objective attitude is extremely important in discussing this subject with the child.
>
> If the parent acts guilty or embarrassed or in any way indicates he is awkward about discussing this subject, the child will reflect that attitude.
>
> If the parent is very emphatic about the rules but uses the same attitude he does when discussing crossing streets or riding bicycles, the child will understand their importance but is not likely to develop any unnatural fears on this subject.
>
> Repetition is important. Every once in a while have your child tell you the rules for strangers.
>
> Be consistent. If you allow a child exceptions to the rules he becomes confused. A child should always have permission to go into someone's house or get into a car.

"Communication is the key," says Sergeant Genevieve Hauck. "If you talk with your child and your child is trusting, you will find out things. And watch his or her changes of behavior. Is your child suddenly reluctant to kiss his father or uncle? Is he afraid of him?"

There are cases of boy friends who go with women only for their daughters. There are leaders of boys' groups, church activities, and physical education who are child molesters. One woman I know recently remarried, but a few years ago she was a divorcee with a nine-year-old son who needed a father figure. This woman, call her Hanna, contacted a local men's group:

> My boy and I met this man. He seemed like a good man, had a fine job, liked boys, and my son liked him. So Saturdays, off they'd go fishing or to ball games or for long walks. My boy was very excited and looked forward all week to his Saturdays with this man.
>
> Then I noticed a change. My son stalled and balked about going off on Saturdays. When he returned at night, he wouldn't tell me about the day. Naturally, I got concerned. I let it ride for a few weeks, but then I sat my boy down and had a talk.
>
> What happened was this so-called upstanding man would treat my boy to all kinds of fun, then they'd get into his car and the man would fondle him. My son knew it was wrong but didn't want to tell me because he thought he'd get the man in trouble.
>
> I told my boy that what this man was doing wasn't right, that this man really shouldn't be among boys. The man needed to see a doctor.

Hanna reported this man to the head of the men's group and, fortunately, the man admitted what he'd done and agreed to consult a psychiatrist. Many child molesters won't admit what they've done, won't voluntarily see a psychiatrist. They say they will but never do. Sergeant Hauck comments, "Report a child molester, even your close relative, because he's sick. He'll undergo psychiatric examination before he's sentenced and might get treatment without imprisonment. But if he's not reported to the authorities, he probably will not get the medical treatment he needs."

When the boy friend, stepfather, or father is molesting a daughter or a son, the mother is often the last to find out. The child will tell a friend before telling her mother because she's afraid, "If I tell, Daddy will go to jail and then we won't have food." Many mothers reason exactly the same way. If the man is in prison, who's going to pay the bills? "Some mothers just talk with the father," says Sergeant Hauck, "and ask him to stop. If he doesn't, she might do nothing. The daughter knows her Mom will side with her Dad so the girl tells a friend or an aunt."

Sooner or later, word gets out. It has to. "A man who will molest his kids will go on to molest other's kids," concludes Sergeant Hauck.

If the child molester is a neighbor, keep the child away. If you can't keep your child away, either have an unemotional talk with the neighbor or contact the police. If the child molester is right in your family, you must see to it that he gets psychiatric attention. He needs help. The police can help you get it for him.

One last point. It is possible to contact the police about a child molester and refrain from giving your name. This will at least alert the police to the problem. You can help the police, your community, and your child much more by cooperating fully with the authorities. Parents are often reluctant to involve their children with the police and are afraid that questioning, identification of the suspect, and a court appearance might frighten them. "This is not usually true," advises the Seattle Police Department. "The child gets satisfaction from helping the police. Juvenile Officers are experienced in talking to the children and know how to approach the subject so that the victim is so engrossed in being an important witness that he tends to be less preoccupied or disturbed over the nature of the offense."

RAPE WITH A PRIOR RELATIONSHIP

In earlier chapters we discussed forcible rape where the offender and the victim didn't know each other at all or only slightly. That is the kind of rape that usually gets to court and stands a good chance of getting the guilty party convicted.

Most rapes, however, occur inside houses and apartments between people who know each other, and are often called "victim-precipitated rapes" or "rapes of a noncautious victim." These labels indicate society's suspicions of a woman who claims to have been raped by someone she knows. The police, the district attorney, the judge, and the jury will first examine her, the supposed victim, and if convinced it was a true rape will then examine the suspect.

"Why?" a woman who has been attacked and raped by someone she knows may well ask.

"Most of the rape reports we get," says Sergeant Lee Kirkwood, "concern a couple who are in a home or a car and have gone so far that when she says, 'No,' he can't or won't stop. She may be fighting with herself, too, for she may both want to stop and to continue."

When a woman is with someone she knows in a situation where there is a potential for intimate relations, it is almost impossible to determine whether or not she was truly raped. Did she consent or not? Was force used or not? Comments one attorney, "Rape is not a fixed point on a line. It is a sliding scale of consent and nonconsent, of force and lack of force."

When alcohol, pot, or other depressants or stimulants are also involved, you may have a hard time remembering exactly what happened. But even if you're sure, you'll have an almost impossible time convincing a jury.

Of course if you are physically harmed and have the cuts and bruises to prove it, people will probably believe you. But whenever there is petting, it is up to the victim to prove that she didn't consent and that intercourse was forced upon her.

"You can prevent this type of crime," says Sergeant Barbara Guarino, "by avoiding the situation. If you can't avoid the situation, be very careful how you conduct yourself."

A woman who is very careful may still find herself involved with someone she knows and likes but doesn't want to be intimate with. If he will not accept "No" and tries to force himself on her, she must act for herself.

Chapter 10 has suggestions for a confrontation with a rapist. Use whatever is appropriate to your situation and you may stop his attack. If not, you can give him the cuts and bruises that will help prove you did not consent and he did use force.

AGGRAVATED ASSAULTS AND MURDER

According to the FBI's *Uniform Crime Reports,* "Most aggravated assaults occur within the family unit, among neighbors or acquaintances. The victim-offender relationship, as well as the very nature of the attack, makes this crime similar to murder."

In 1972 there were 388,650 aggravated assaults, an increase of 7 per cent over the previous year to 187 victims per 100,000 persons. There were also 18,520 murders committed in the United States, an increase of 5 per cent over the previous year to 8.9 victims per 100,000 persons.

But what do all these figures mean? Rick and Sally know. Rick was at a barbecue with Sally, his wife, and some friends when one of the friends turned to Sally and told her she looked pretty. Rick became furious:

> I didn't do anything at the barbecue. No, not then. But when we got home, I said to her, "What were you and him talking about?" She didn't answer me directly and I started to get angry. Real angry. I called her a whole lot of names, bad names. She started yelling at me, saying I didn't trust her, didn't believe in her.
>
> I went out of my mind, out of my gourd, mad, just like a madman. I don't know what got into me. Sometimes I flip, from easygoing to mad. I just couldn't control myself. I started hitting her, beating on her. Messed her up pretty bad.
>
> I think about it now and I feel like a dog, like a mangy dog. I love that woman but I beat up on her. I get so out of my head sometimes, I don't know what gets into me. I just can't control myself. I get so jealous, so crazy. I don't know what to do. I really don't know what to do.

When Rick said these words, Sally sat next to him with a black-and-blue eye and a few cuts on her face. Although she hates his violent streak, Sally loves Rick. "He's hard-working, has a big heart, and is very kind." She didn't feel that way five years ago when he beat her up so bad she landed in the hospital and he was taken to prison. But she was there when he got out and she's still there.

Most family disputes never get beyond the yelling stage, but some, like that of Rick and Sally, are very serious. The police department of New York City used to have a Family Crisis Intervention Unit that responded to calls of family fights. Officials from this unit state, "Family crises are not merely a phenomenon of the lower-class neighborhood, they cut across socio-economic lines and touch every strata of society with violence and sorrow."

Whether they are between husband and wife or parents and off-spring, minor squabbles can lead to major violence. Simi, California, is a community of 70,000 people with an advanced program for dealing with family disputes. A key administrator of the program says, "Small problems boil for years and can end up in murder."

Oakland's Chief of Police C. R. Gain has both figures and one major cause of murders within the family:

> At the very heart of the violent threat to life in America is the domestic dispute. There is no single greater source of homicide. In the city of Oakland, family disputes accounted for 52.9 per cent of the homicides for 1970. . . . The Oakland ex-perience is consistent with the national pattern.
>
> The elimination of handgun ownership will not, of course, prevent the use of violence in domestic disputes, but it is ap-parent from FBI statistics that the alternate weapon choice in domestic disputes would be the knife, not the long gun. This is particularly important when one realizes that a knife is only one seventh as deadly as the gun. In other words, elimination of the handgun from private ownership would not eliminate domestic murders but it would greatly reduce them.

One way you can prevent family squabbles from flaring into murder is to get rid of the handguns you may have in your home. There are additional ways to prevent crimes within the family.

The case of Rick and Sally illustrates another major cause of aggravated assault and murder. I was present when Rick and Sally poured their hearts out to Rick's parole agent. Although Rick claimed, "I really don't know what to do," the parole agent knew better. Rick has a drinking problem. He has great difficulty accepting the fact that just one or two bottles of beer drive him out of his mind. Says the parole agent, "Alcohol is involved in a great many crimes. It is Rick's problem, it is the problem of many people who won't admit it."

If such a problem exists in your home, get rid of the alcohol. In the short run, that act could stop a crime.

Also in the short run, you can prevent some crimes within the family by a very simple method. Says Lieutenant Jim Motherway of New York, "If your spouse wants to argue, don't. Just walk away. Argue and it can escalate, but walk away and there won't be any violence."

Long-term solutions to the passions that lead to violence are discussed by an official of Simi, California. "In the year and a half we've been in operation, we've counseled some 10 per cent of the teen-age population and have arranged for a great many adults to have various counseling services."

Depending upon the specific problem, one or another form of counseling is the best long-term prevention for crimes within the family.

But what if your community doesn't have the centralized services of Simi, California? Go to someone who can find help for you. The people and agencies who can help you include:

A local pastor	Drug clinics
A psychiatrist or psychologist	Free clinics
The police	An ombudsman
Family counseling service	A citizens assistance program
Welfare Department	A citizens advocacy program
Mental health agencies	The mayor's office
Alcohol counseling, including	
Alcoholics Anonymous	

The names for various organizations vary, but if there's no obvious group to call, take a few minutes and try two or three of the above. Be prepared to be bounced around a little. When you're trying to avert a tragedy within your family, a few minutes and some bouncing around are well worth it.

You are the only person who can prevent a crime within your family. After they have been alerted, the police or a pastor or a psychiatrist or some other party can help, but the call for help must be made by you. It's your family.

14

Who Will Be a Victim?

The mayor of a major eastern city was driving home one night recently when he stopped at a red light with his left hand outside the window. A pedestrian crossing the street saw the watch on the mayor's wrist, rushed over, grabbed the watch and ran off.

In another city, a woman carefully locked all the doors of her apartment, then stepped into her bathroom to take a quiet bath. As she lay back in the warm water, suddenly the medicine cabinet leaped off the wall and a strange man stuck his head through the opening.

This man had just burglarized the apartment next door and planned to plunder her home by prying off the medicine cabinet and climbing through the hole in the wall.

Meanwhile, a young woman in a sports car sat at the side of a highway. Her car had broken down. No phones or police were nearby and she was very concerned for her safety until she saw a tow truck pull up behind her. As she hadn't called it, she thought herself very lucky the tow truck had come from out of nowhere.

The driver looked at her car, said he could tow it or put in a minor part and she could drive away. She asked him to fix it; he said he could get the part at a nearby gas station. She could stay with the car or come with him. She went with him and has never been heard from again.

The case histories of the mayor and the woman in the bathtub are factual. The young woman in the broken-down car has never been heard from and police think she was picked up by a man in a roving tow truck.

The moral of these three stories is the moral of this entire book: be alert, be aware, beware. Or in the words of a Detroit expert, "Always be aware that danger can exist."

Even while taking a bath. Fortunately, the woman in the bathtub laughed about her experience as she talked about it later. After all, she had taken several security precautions. But she didn't laugh when that strange man stuck his head through the opening in the wall.

Remember the woman in the bathtub or the mayor at the stoplight or the young woman at the side of the road next time you leave your house. These people didn't expect the unexpected. You will be safer if you do.

By expecting the unexpected, you will be psychologically prepared for just about any eventuality. By being psychologically prepared, you may even prevent crime from happening to you because you will look alert.

From my interviews with over two dozen different convicted felons, one similarity among almost all of their victims stands out: the victim offered the offender an *opportunity*. Whether it was a door unlocked, a car window rolled down, keys in the car, a note on the front door, a pocketbook held by the straps, a little girl walking home by herself, a young woman hitchhiking, a mother not watching the rearview mirror of her car as she drove home— whether it was one of these or some other opportunity, these men took advantage of it and of the women and little girls.

You must act for yourself and for those you love because the police simply can't be everywhere at the same time. They can't be both outside patrolling the streets and inside watching apartment buildings and houses. While the police are helping you by patrolling your community, you must help yourself.

You are safer if you also help the police:

> Crime is a community problem.
>
> For a long time, people expected the police to assume the responsibility for all that is criminal. But today crime has outgrown the expected boundaries and has become a problem in every neighborhood and on every street.
>
> It is the most serious challenge of our generation.
>
> Now we are asking—very directly—for your help.

Those are the words of a top Dallas official as he launched a neighborhood crime-prevention program called "Operation: Get Involved." There are similar programs in Los Angeles, Philadelphia, Newton, Massachusetts, and many other cities and towns. Check with your police department; they can help you; you can help them.

There are other things you can do to control crime where you live. If you've got the money, you can get together with your neighbors and hire a security patrol. Many companies that provide security guards for businesses are now offering their services to apartment buildings and homeowners. Look in the Yellow Pages under guard and patrol services for a selection of different agencies.

Although these guards will patrol your apartment building or neighborhood, they take only a little of the responsibility off your shoulders. If you provide an opportunity when at home or while walking or driving or riding in public transportation, then you may become a victim.

To combat crime, you can participate in a tenants association, a block parent program, Operation Identification, or a community-police program such as the Basic Car Plan (Los Angeles), the Beat Committee (Dallas), or other regular meetings of the community and the police in your area.

In 1967 a group of women who were concerned about crime in Atlanta met with some of the city's crime-prevention officers. Today there are Crime Prevention Clubs in eleven different areas of Atlanta. An expert with the Atlanta Crime Prevention Bureau comments, "It is the contention of the Crime Prevention Bureau that every crime committed in this city of Atlanta is known by someone else other than the perpetrator. We have simply made requests to the public to assist in cleaning up crime in their communities and the response has been tremendous."

In this Atlanta program, the women, and now the men also, send anonymous letters to the police with information on crimes. As drugs are a major cause of crime, there are other programs in other areas of the country to dry up drugs. One of the most successful is called TIP (for Turn In Pushers) and is found in Fairfax, Virginia. About $300 is offered for the arrest and conviction of drug pushers. As this is written, police have received one hundred leads and from these have had ninety-nine arrests and convictions. These are some of the programs you can help set up in your community.

Here's another: about two years ago, some women in New Orleans got fed up with the rates of burglary and forcible rape that surpassed those of New York and Chicago. So they formed Women Against Crime. They now have 4,000 volunteers throughout the city watching neighborhoods and meeting with neighbors, teaching people how to protect their homes from burglary and themselves from purse snatching and rape. Burglaries and rapes are "down drastically" in New Orleans now.

There's much you can do to fight crime in your community. If you want to cop out and blame our crime problems on inefficient courts, judges who are too lenient, penal institutions that don't rehabilitate, or police who are not effective, then you are only hurting yourself. Although there are serious problems with our court and penal systems, and although many of our police departments are understaffed and underequipped, there is much that *you* can do. You can work with the police, with neighbors, with groups you already belong to, with local, state, and federal government agencies, with church groups, social groups, political groups.

Fighting crime starts at home, includes your immediate neighbors, and extends throughout your community. No matter how much or how little you are able and willing to do, remember the words of Chief of Police Jerry V. Wilson of Washington, D.C. "Everyone can help reduce crime; prevention is the key."

Who will be a victim? The person who gives crime an opportunity, who is not alert and aware, who is not psychologically prepared, who is not expecting the unexpected—this person will be a victim.

Would you trust the man on the following page?

This is Bob Lucente. He's not a drug addict or a hippie, he's a policeman. He works undercover in New York.

6/11/15

DISCARD